Christmas Favorites for Solo Jazz Guitar

Arranged by Paul Pappas

CONTENTS

Cherry Lane Music
Director of Publications/Project Editor: Mark Phillips

ISBN 978-1-57560-791-7

ANGELS WE HAVE HEARD ON HIGH

French-English

Moderately slow Swing (♩♩ = ♩ ♪ triplet)

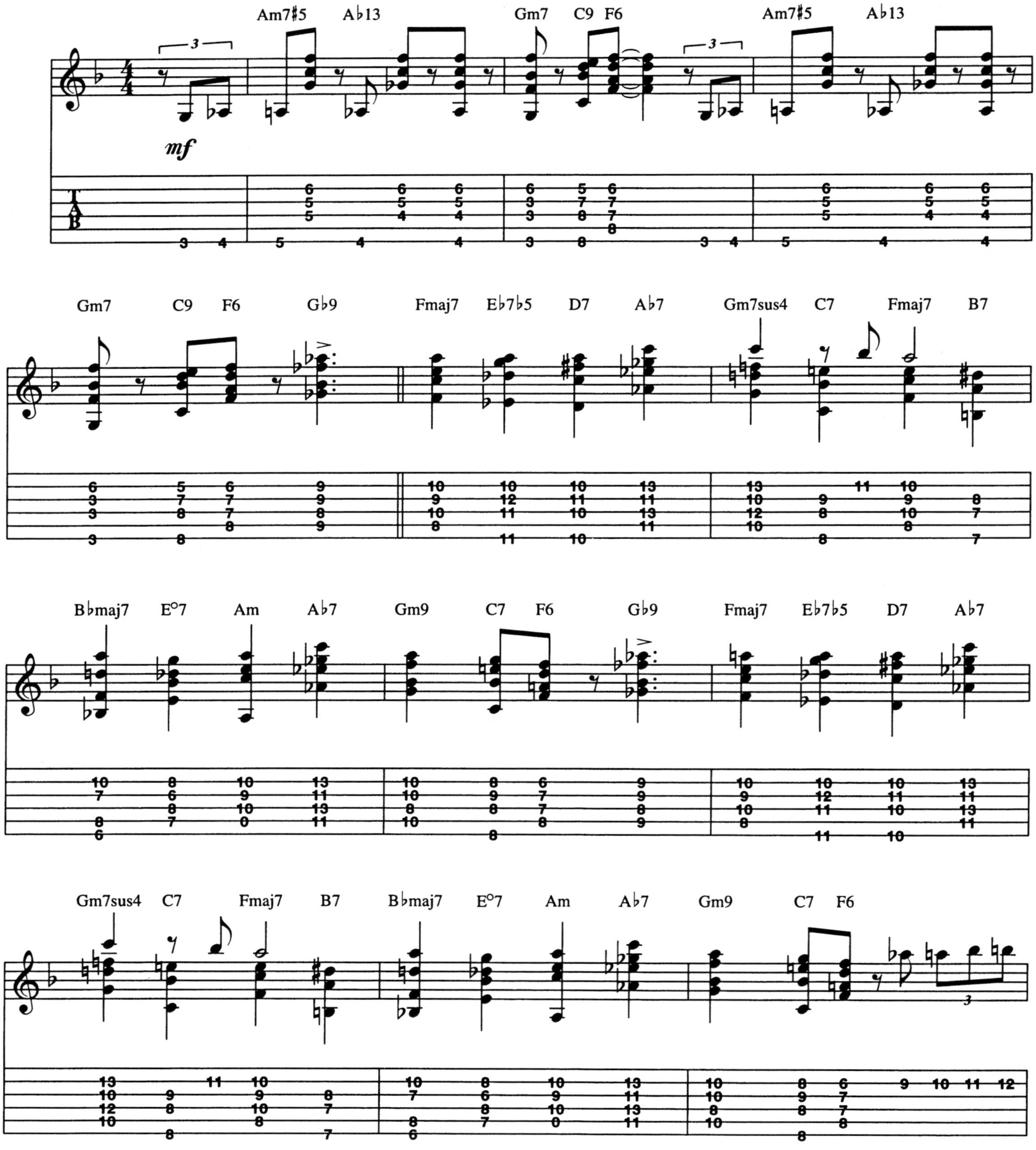

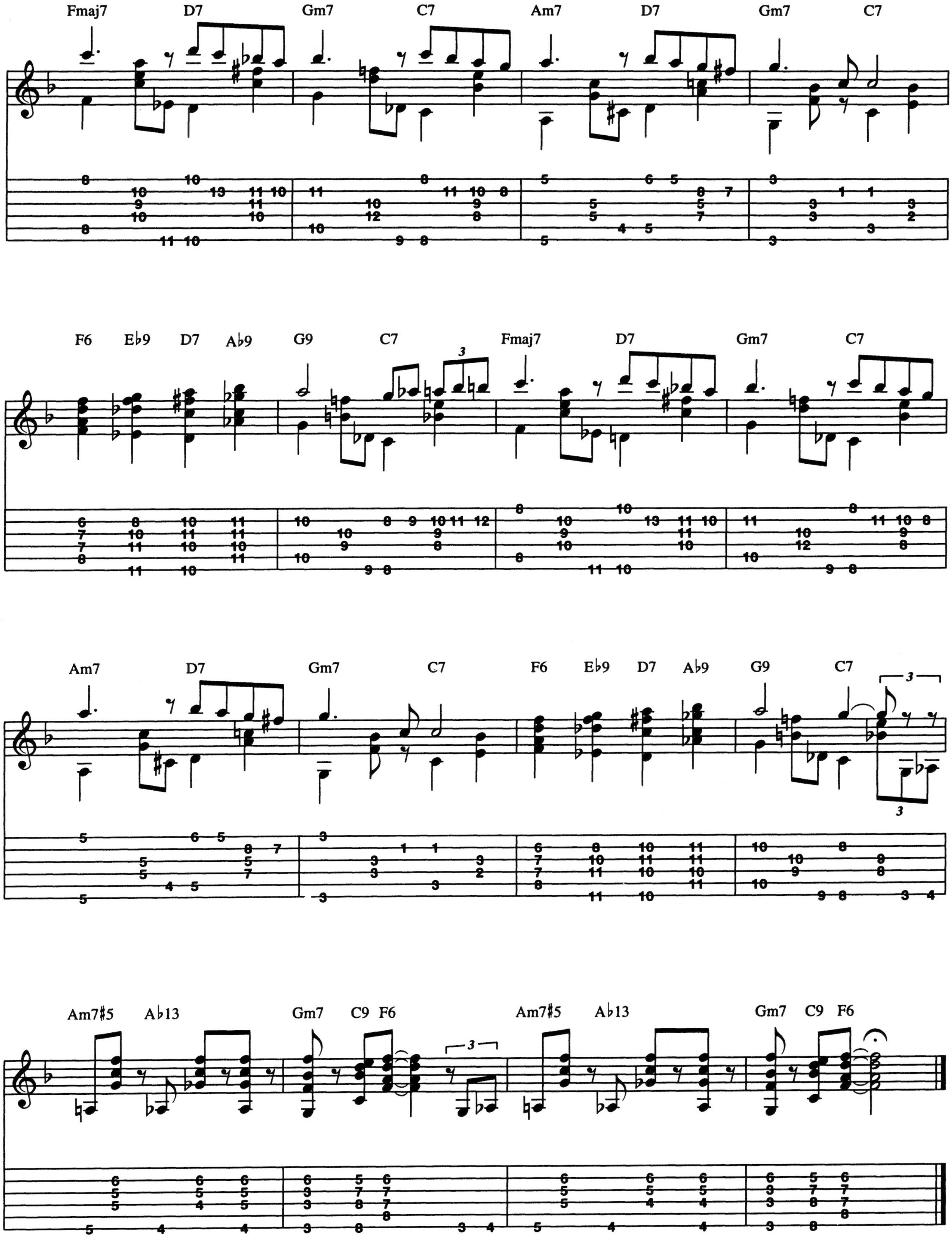
Fmaj7 D7 Gm7 C7 Am7 D7 Gm7 C7
F6 E♭9 D7 A♭9 G9 C7 Fmaj7 D7 Gm7 C7
Am7 D7 Gm7 C7 F6 E♭9 D7 A♭9 G9 C7
Am7♯5 A♭13 Gm7 C9 F6 Am7♯5 A♭13 Gm7 C9 F6

AWAY IN A MANGER

Music attributed to James R. Murray

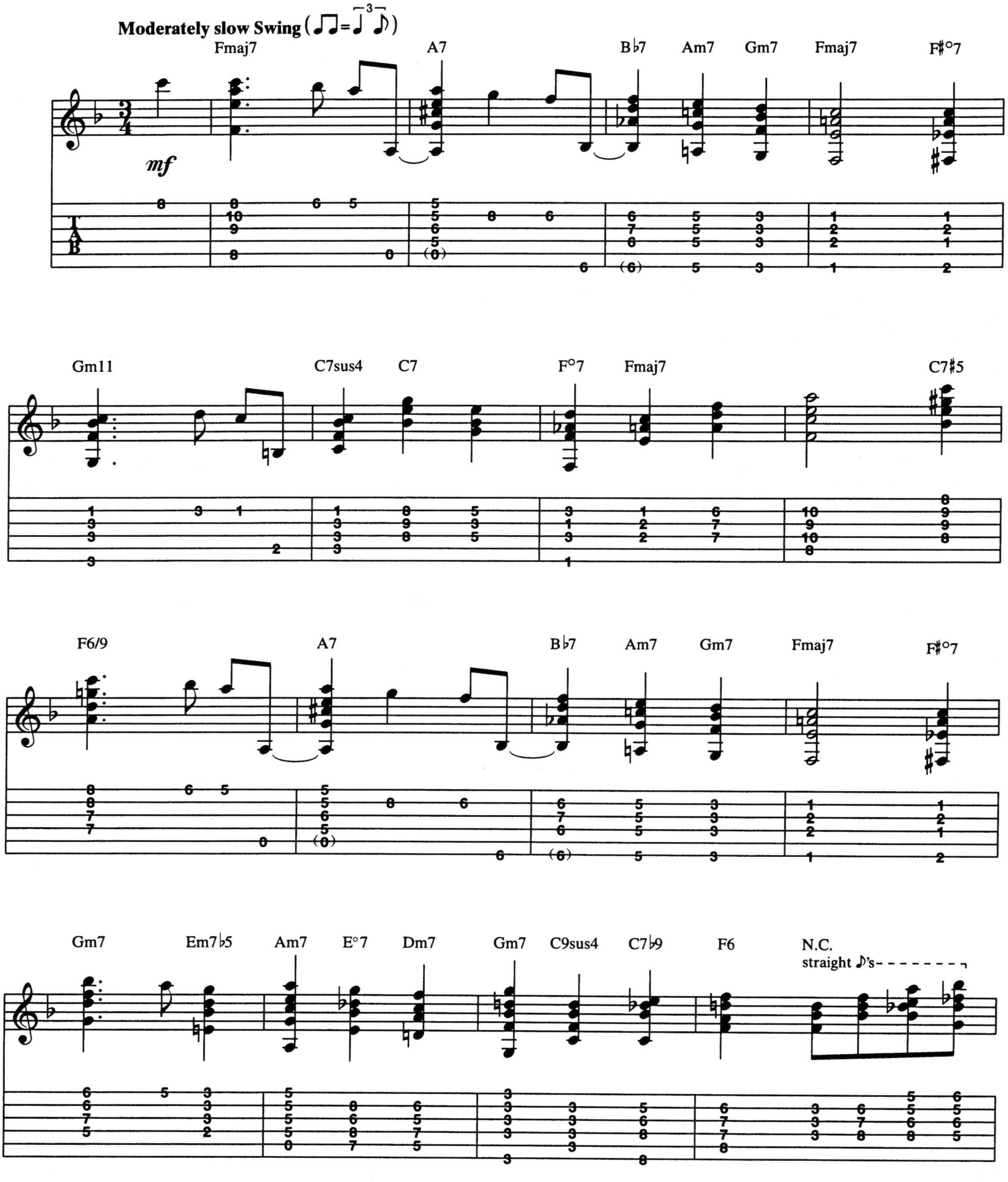

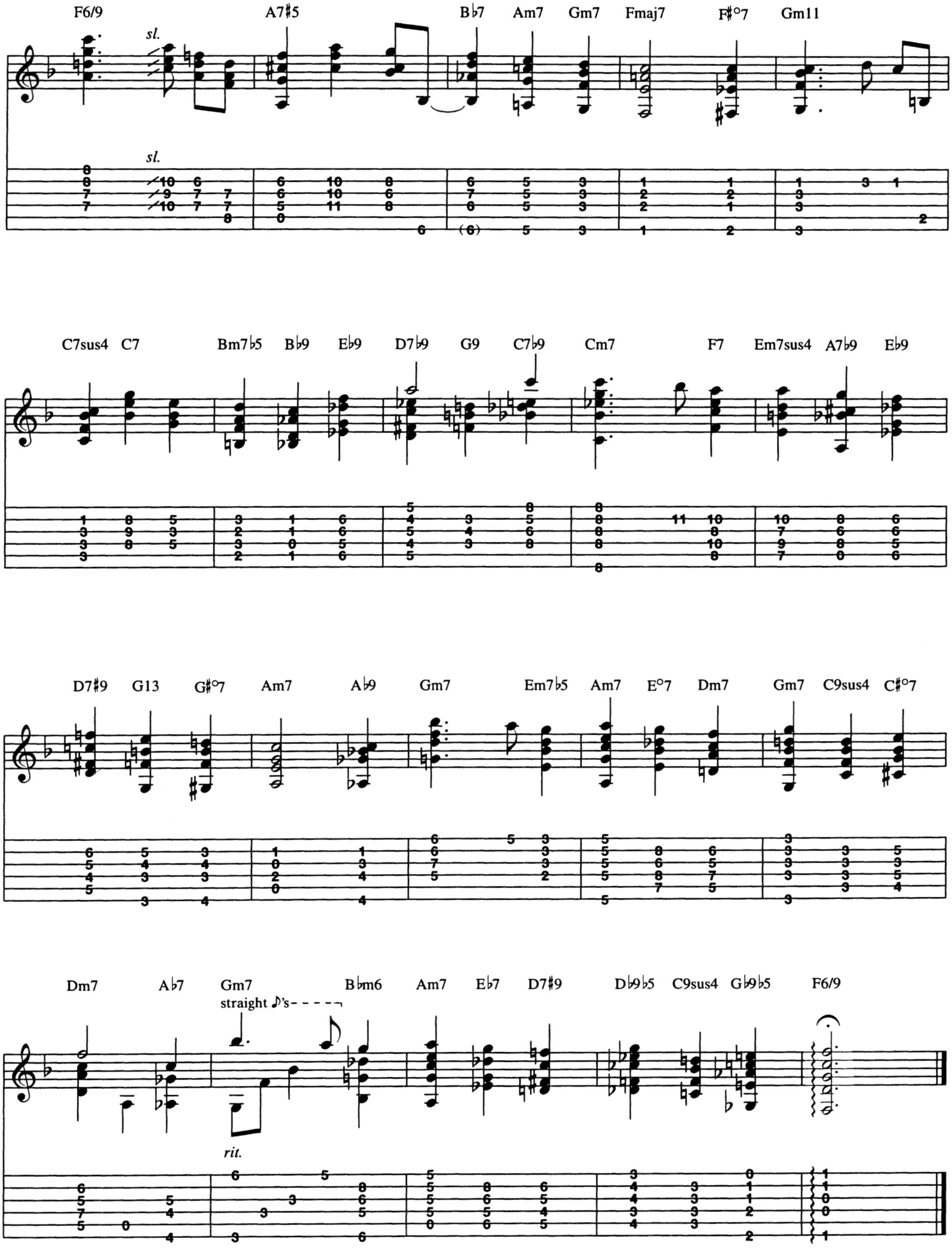
F6/9 A7♯5 B♭7 Am7 Gm7 Fmaj7 F♯°7 Gm11
sl.
C7sus4 C7 Bm7♭5 B♭9 E♭9 D7♭9 G9 C7♭9 Cm7 F7 Em7sus4 A7♭9 E♭9
D7♯9 G13 G♯°7 Am7 A♭9 Gm7 Em7♭5 Am7 E°7 Dm7 Gm7 C9sus4 C♯°7
Dm7 A♭7 Gm7 B♭m6 Am7 E♭7 D7♯9 D♭9♭5 C9sus4 G♭9♭5 F6/9
straight ♪'s
rit.

DECK THE HALLS

Old Welsh

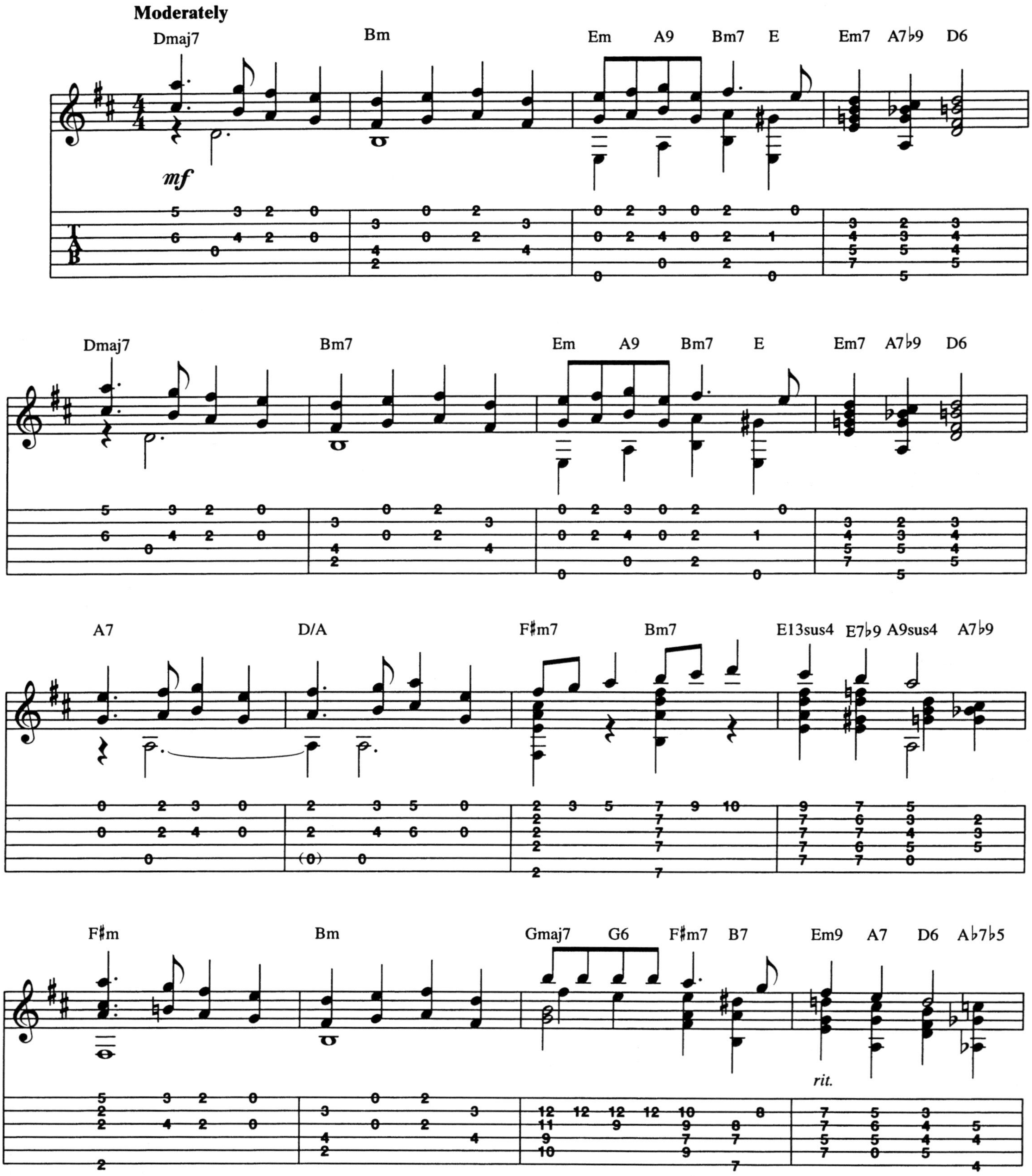

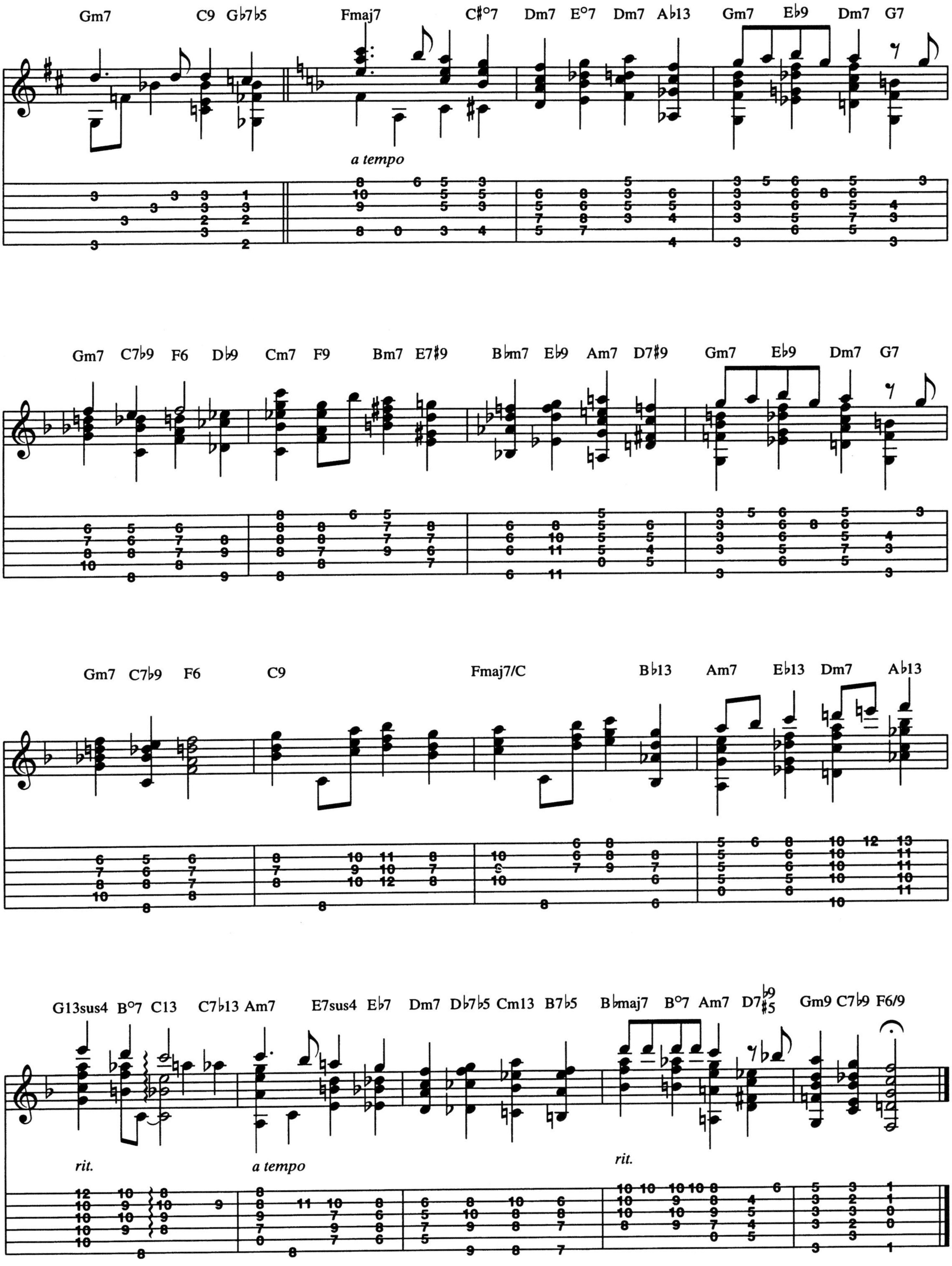
Gm7 C9 G♭7♭5 Fmaj7 C♯°7 Dm7 E°7 Dm7 A♭13 Gm7 E♭9 Dm7 G7
a tempo
Gm7 C7♭9 F6 D♭9 Cm7 F9 Bm7 E7♯9 B♭m7 E♭9 Am7 D7♯9 Gm7 E♭9 Dm7 G7
Gm7 C7♭9 F6 C9 Fmaj7/C B♭13 Am7 E♭13 Dm7 A♭13
G13sus4 B°7 C13 C7♭13 Am7 E7sus4 E♭7 Dm7 D♭7♭5 Cm13 B7♭5 B♭maj7 B°7 Am7 D7♭9♯5 Gm9 C7♭9 F6/9
rit.
a tempo
rit.

GOD REST YE MERRY, GENTLEMEN

Traditional English

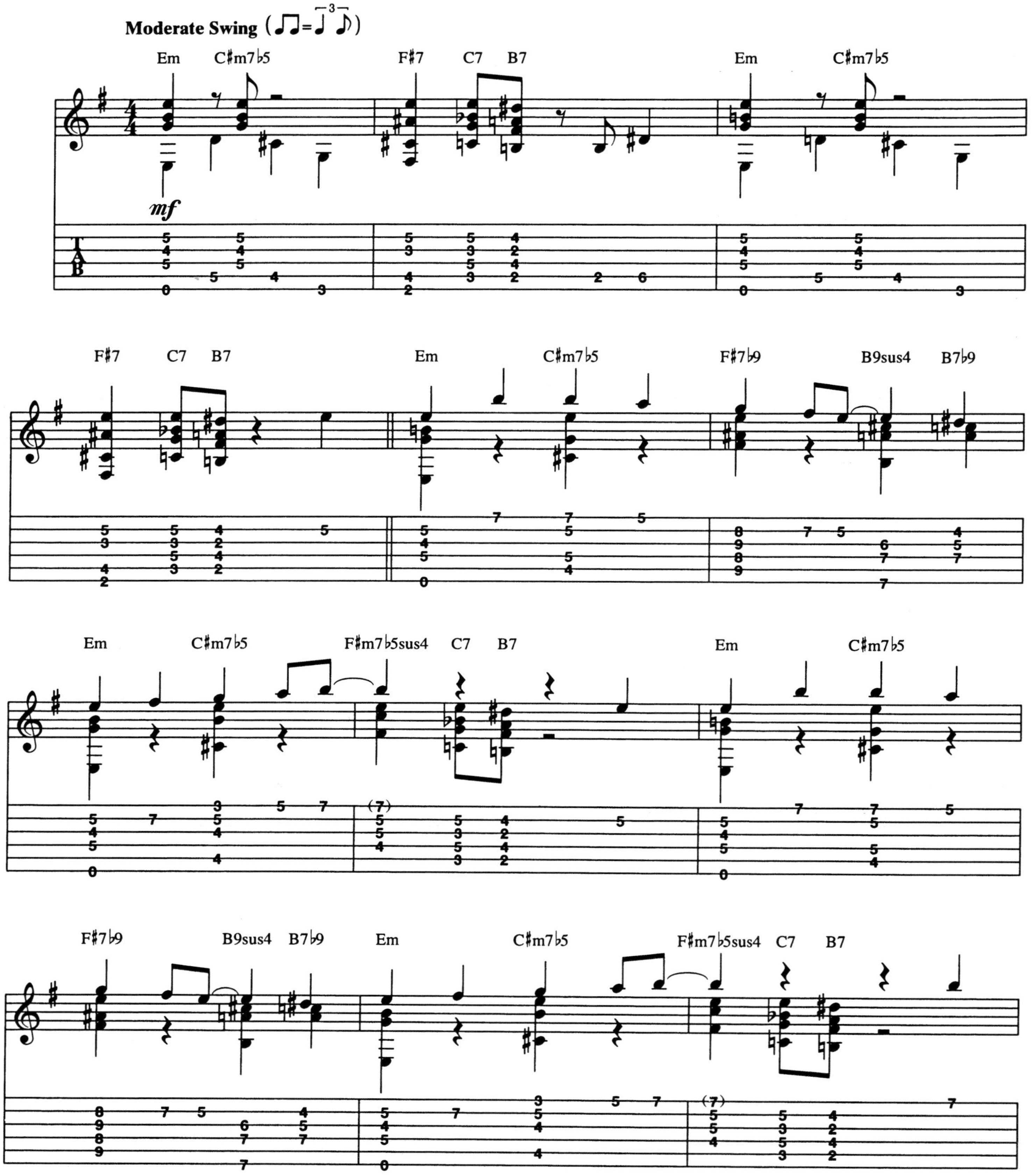

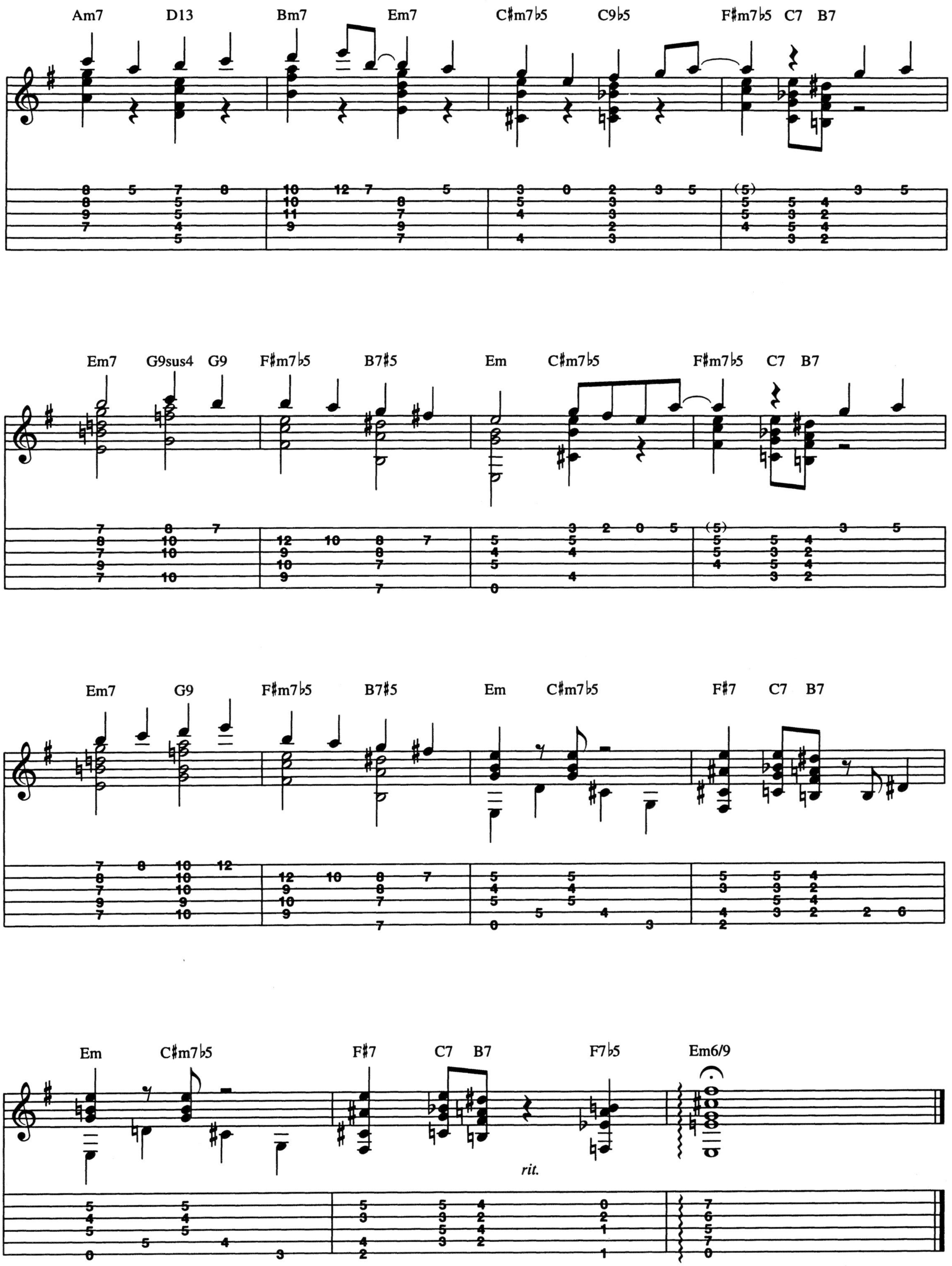
Am7 D13 Bm7 Em7 C#m7♭5 C9♭5 F#m7♭5 C7 B7
Em7 G9sus4 G9 F#m7♭5 B7#5 Em C#m7♭5 F#m7♭5 C7 B7
Em7 G9 F#m7♭5 B7#5 Em C#m7♭5 F#7 C7 B7
Em C#m7♭5 F#7 C7 B7 F7♭5 Em6/9
rit.

GOOD KING WENCESLAS

Words by John Mason Neale
English Folk Melody

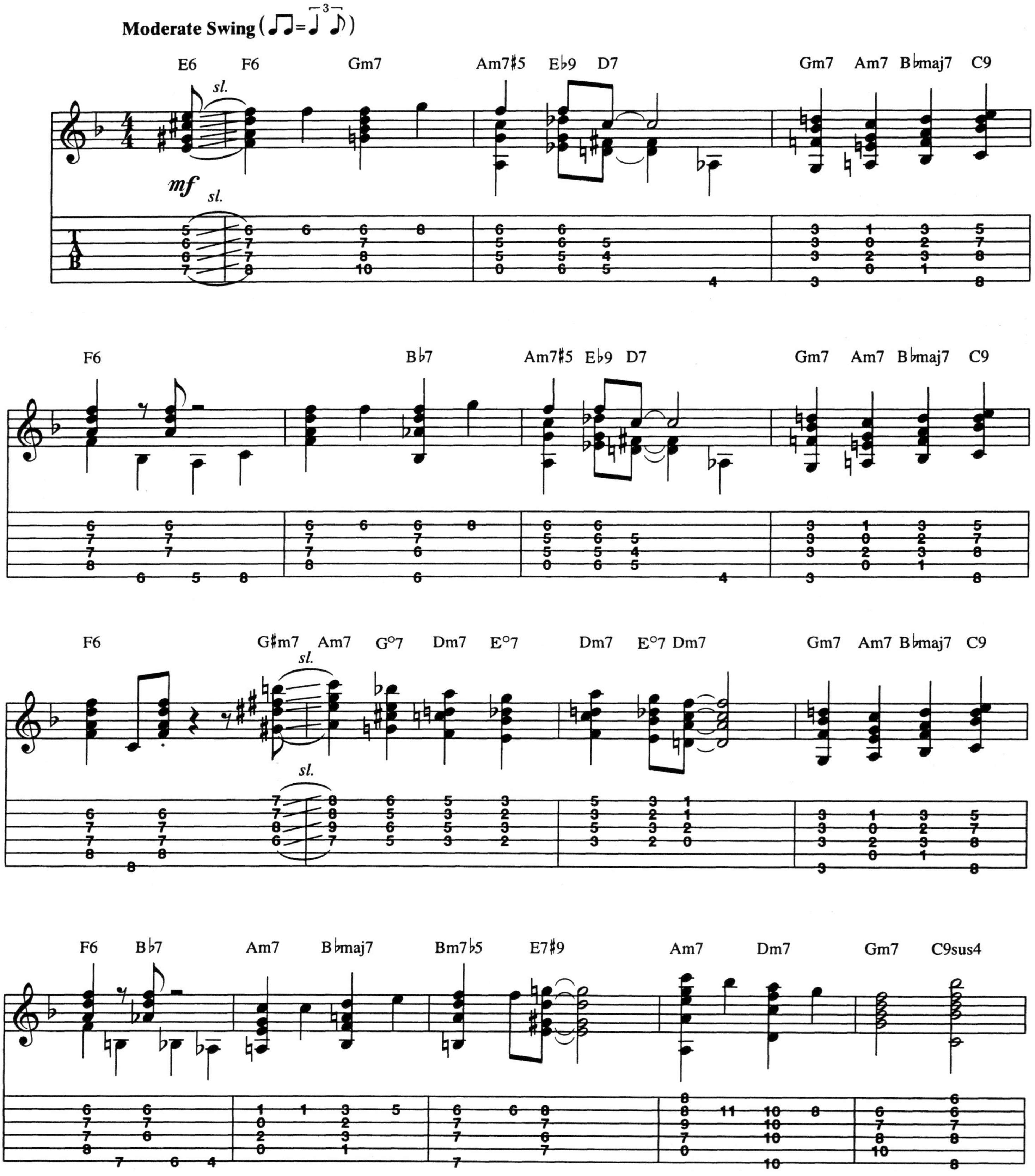

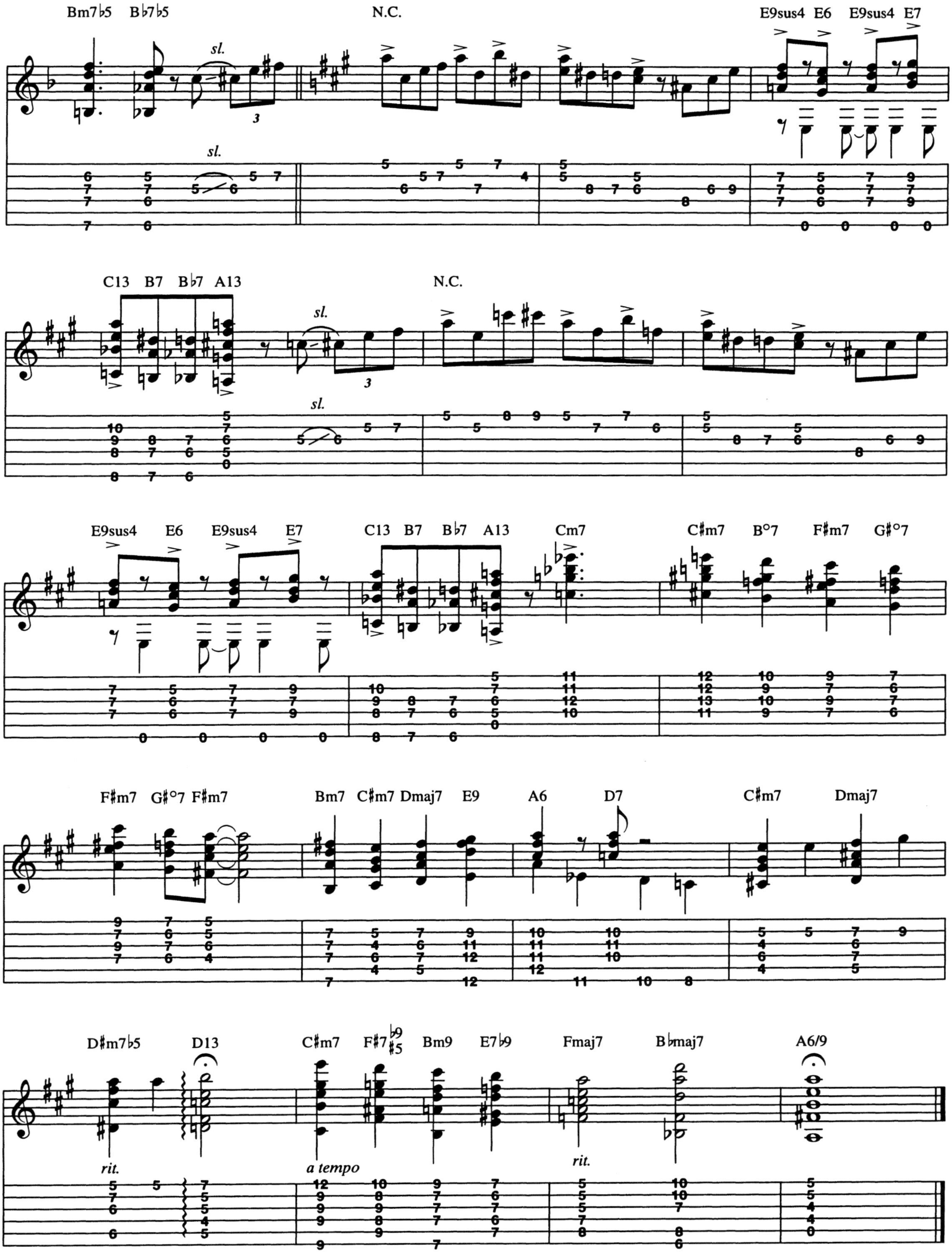
Bm7♭5 B♭7♭5 N.C. E9sus4 E6 E9sus4 E7
sl.
C13 B7 B♭7 A13 N.C.
sl.
E9sus4 E6 E9sus4 E7 C13 B7 B♭7 A13 Cm7 C♯m7 B°7 F♯m7 G♯°7
F♯m7 G♯°7 F♯m7 Bm7 C♯m7 Dmaj7 E9 A6 D7 C♯m7 Dmaj7
D♯m7♭5 D13 C♯m7 F♯7♭9♯5 Bm9 E7♭9 Fmaj7 B♭maj7 A6/9
rit.
a tempo
rit.

HARK! THE HERALD ANGELS SING

Words by Charles Wesley
Music by Felix Mendelssohn-Bartholdy

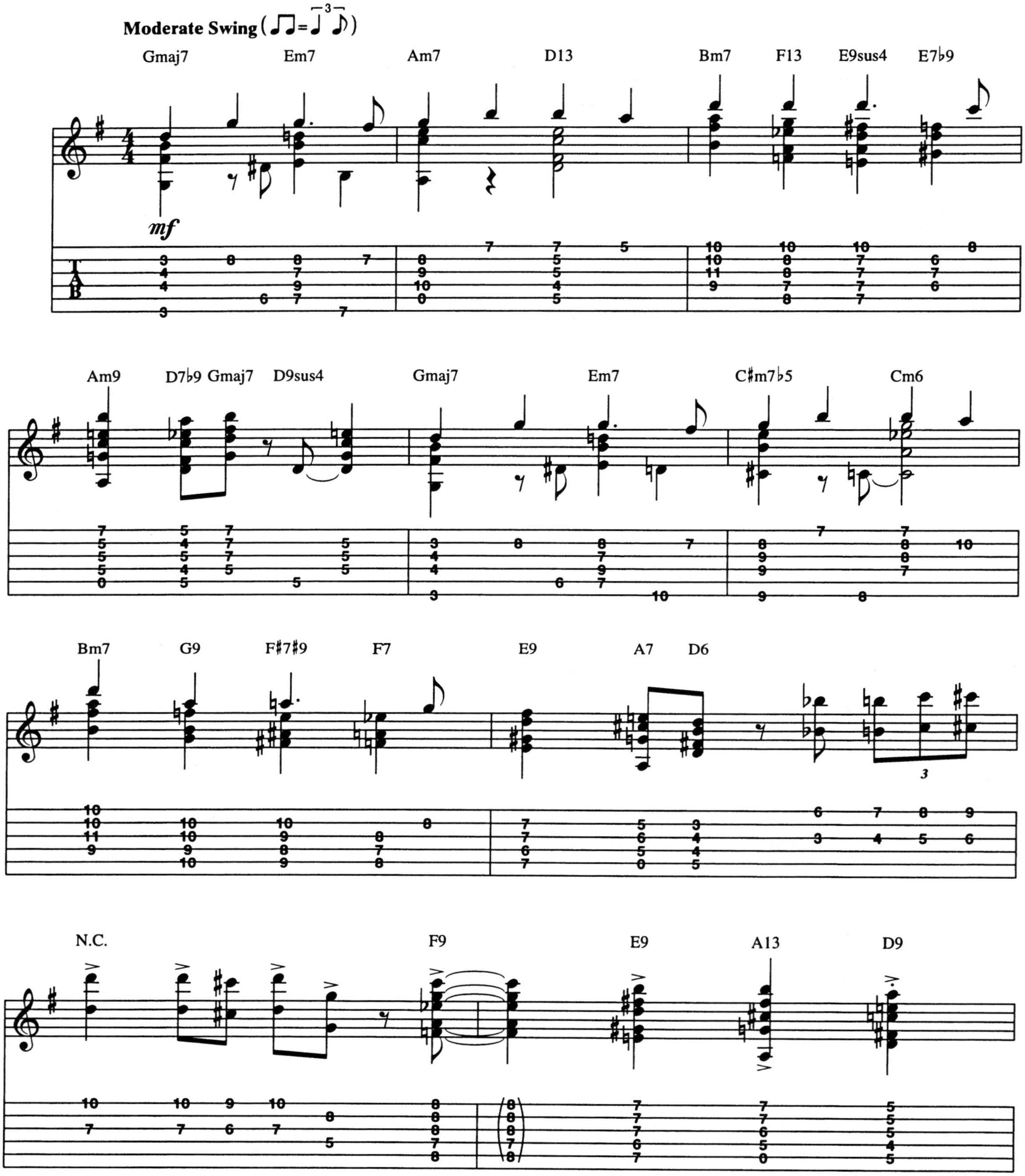

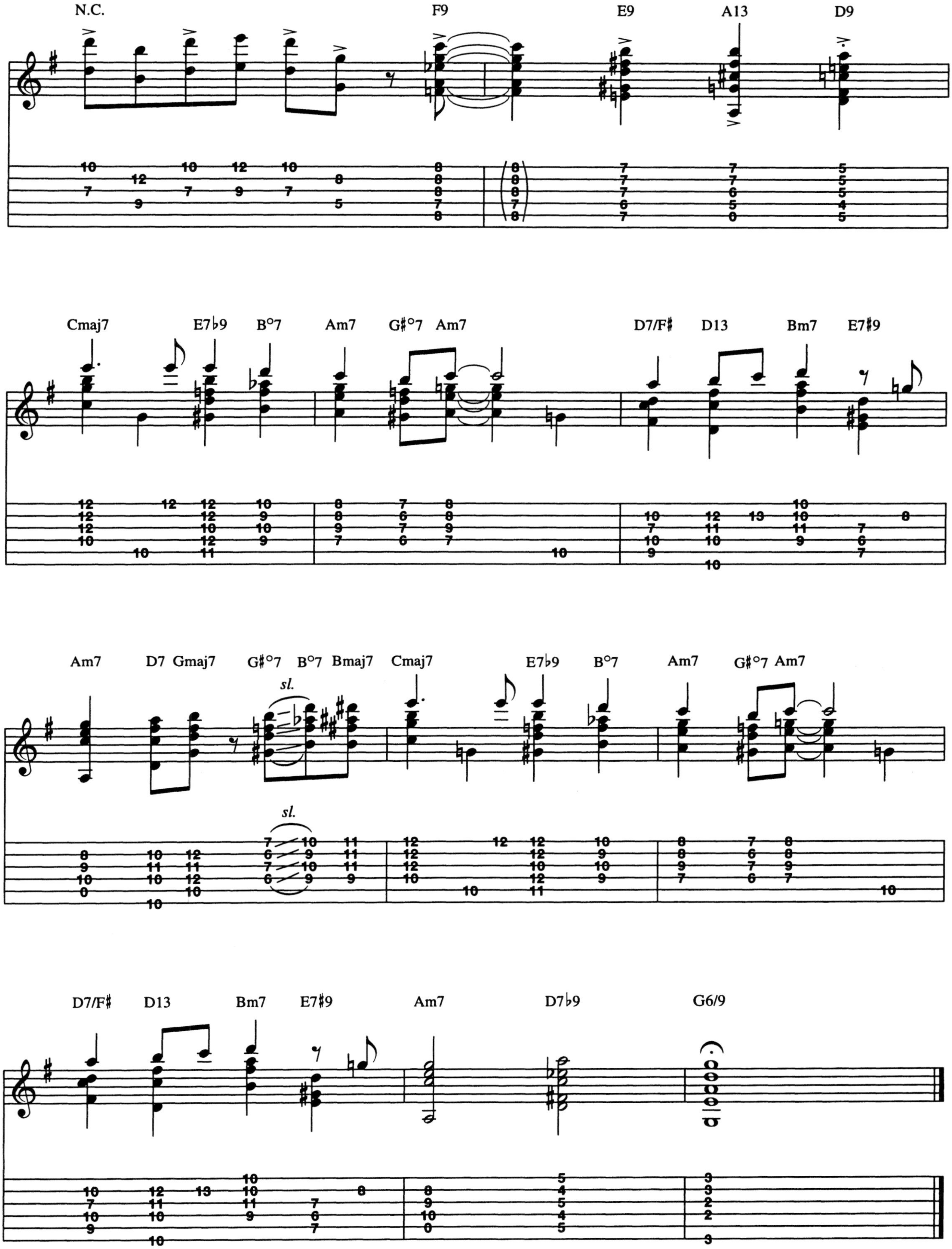
N.C. F9 E9 A13 D9
Cmaj7 E7♭9 B°7 Am7 G♯°7 Am7 D7/F♯ D13 Bm7 E7♯9
Am7 D7 Gmaj7 G♯°7 B°7 Bmaj7 Cmaj7 E7♭9 B°7 Am7 G♯°7 Am7
sl.
sl.
D7/F♯ D13 Bm7 E7♯9 Am7 D7♭9 G6/9

It Came Upon a Midnight Clear

Words by Edmund H. Sears
Music by Richard S. Willis

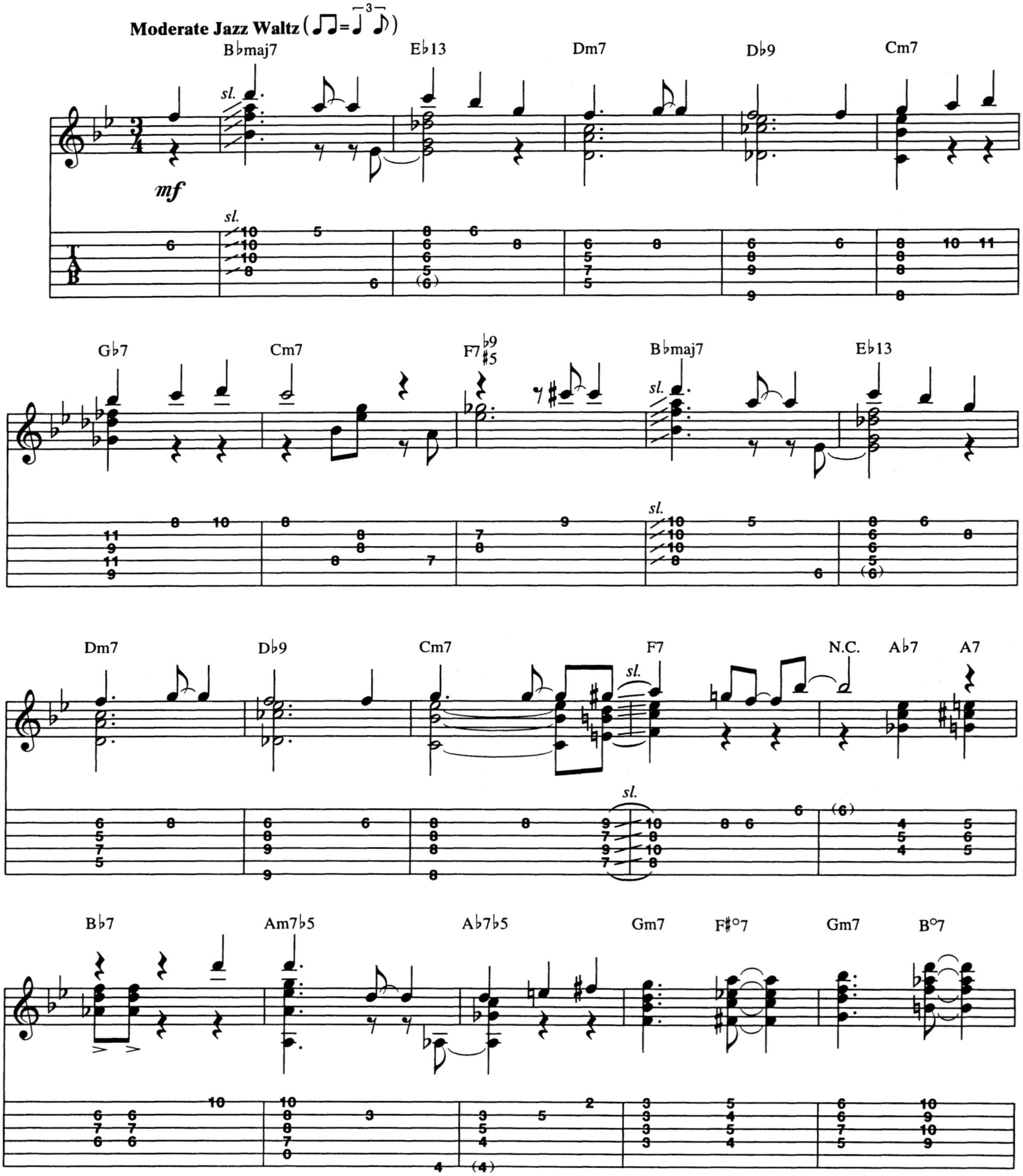

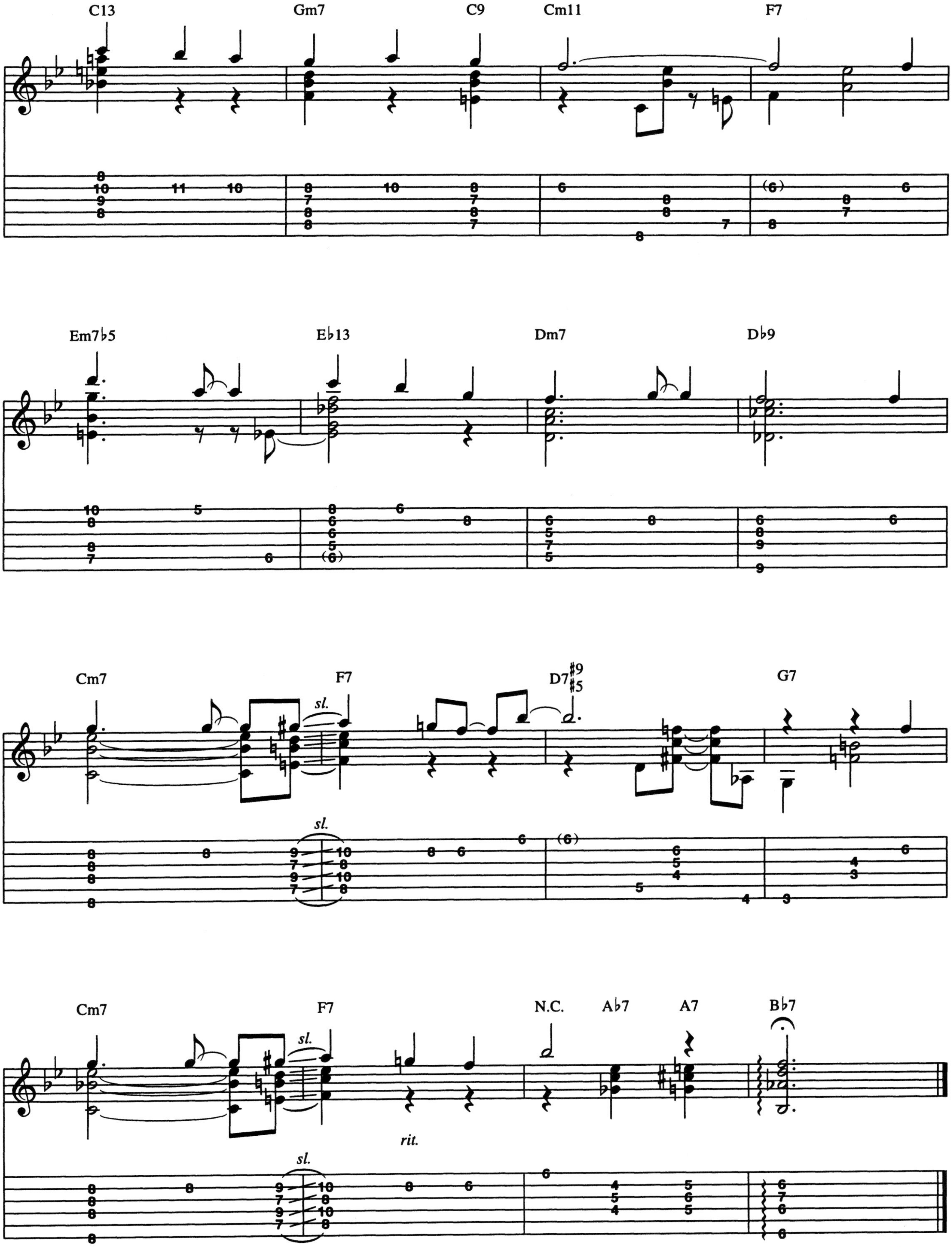
C13
Gm7
C9
Cm11
F7
Em7♭5
E♭13
Dm7
D♭9
Cm7
F7
sl.
D7#9#5
G7
Cm7
F7
sl.
N.C.
A♭7
A7
B♭7
rit.

JINGLE BELLS

Words and Music by John Pierpont

Uptempo Swing

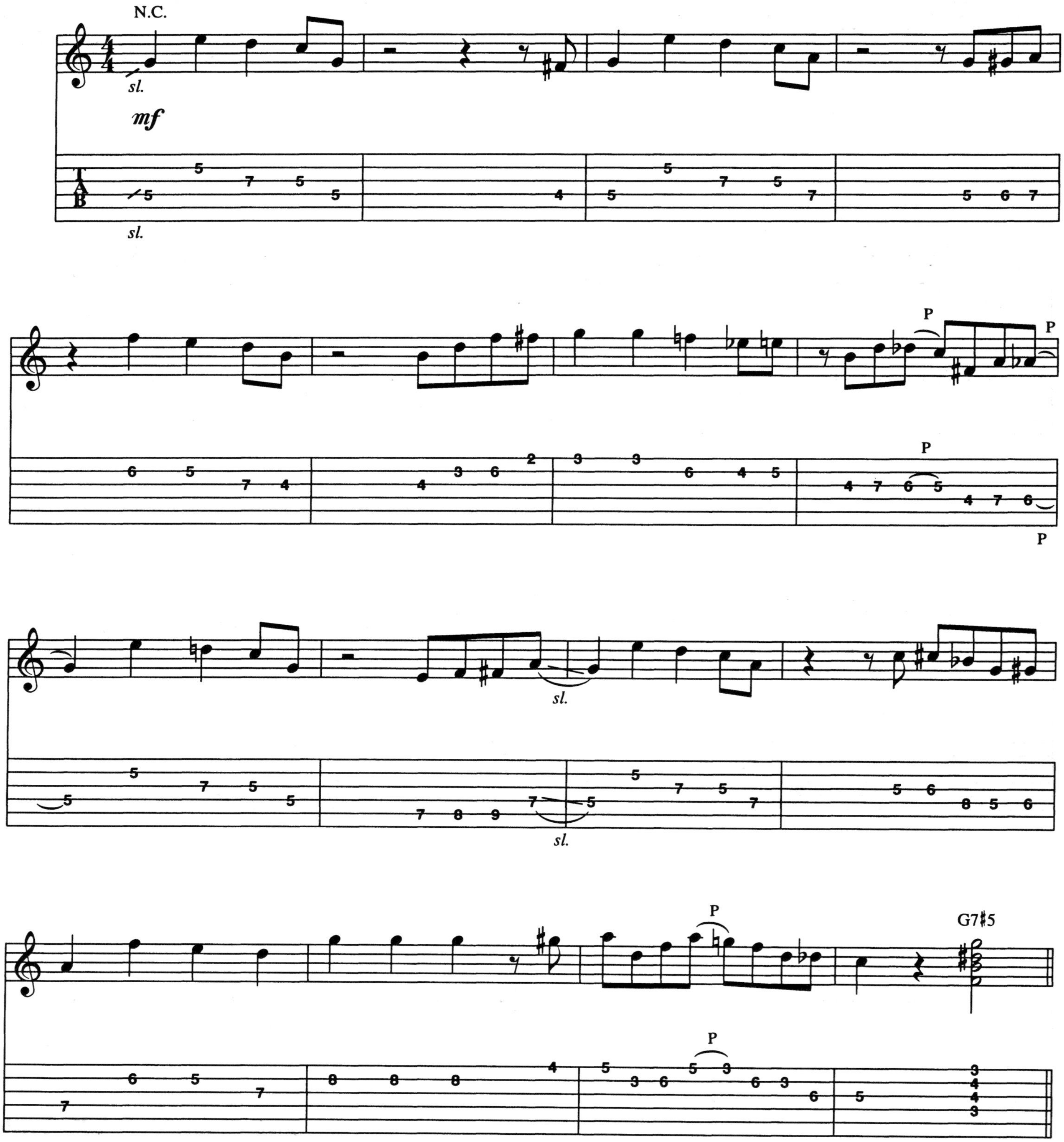

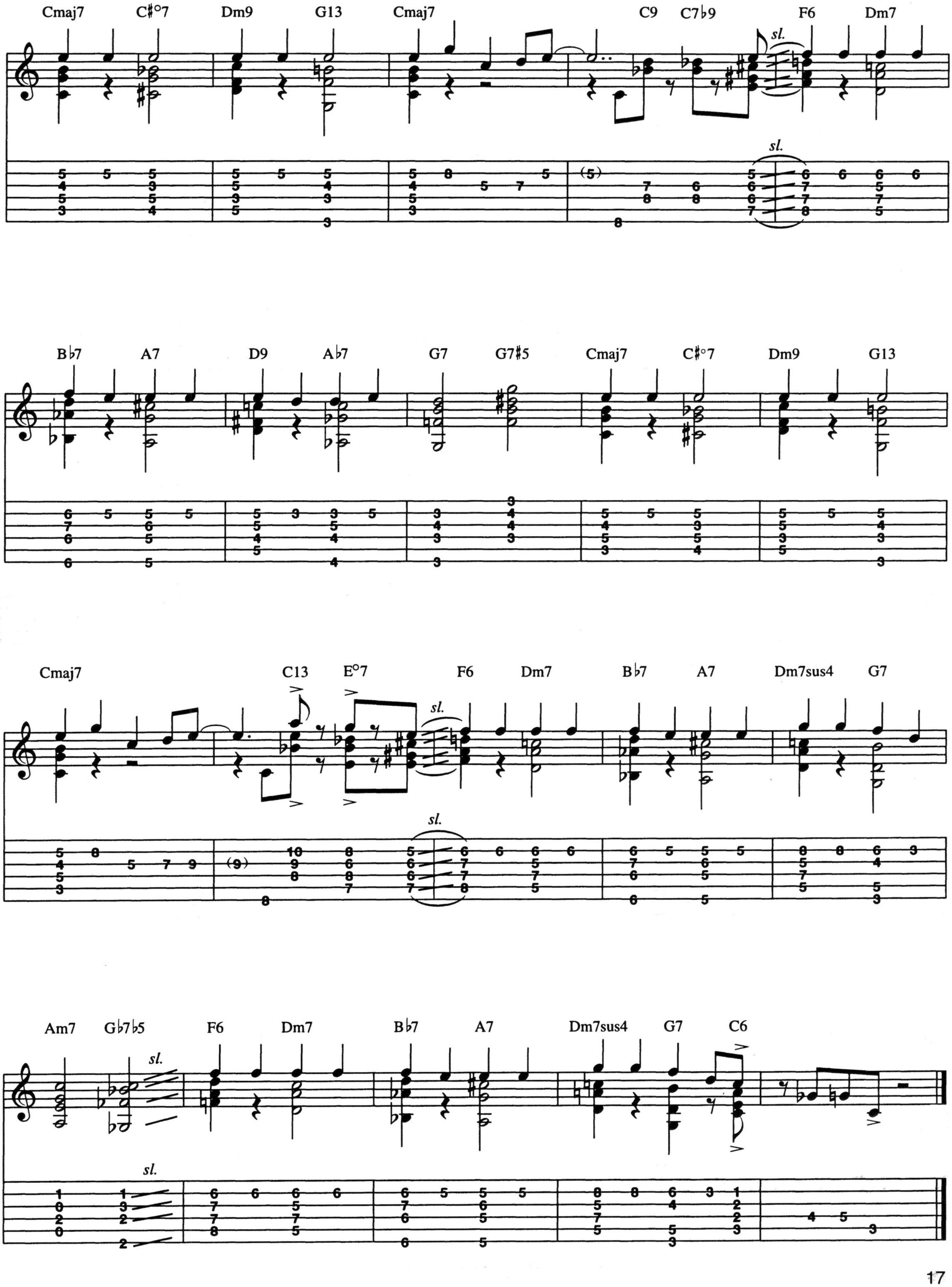
Cmaj7 C♯°7 Dm9 G13 Cmaj7 C9 C7♭9 F6 Dm7
sl.
B♭7 A7 D9 A♭7 G7 G7♯5 Cmaj7 C♯°7 Dm9 G13
Cmaj7 C13 E°7 F6 Dm7 B♭7 A7 Dm7sus4 G7
sl.
Am7 G♭7♭5 F6 Dm7 B♭7 A7 Dm7sus4 G7 C6
sl.

O COME ALL YE FAITHFUL

Words and Music by
John Francis Wade

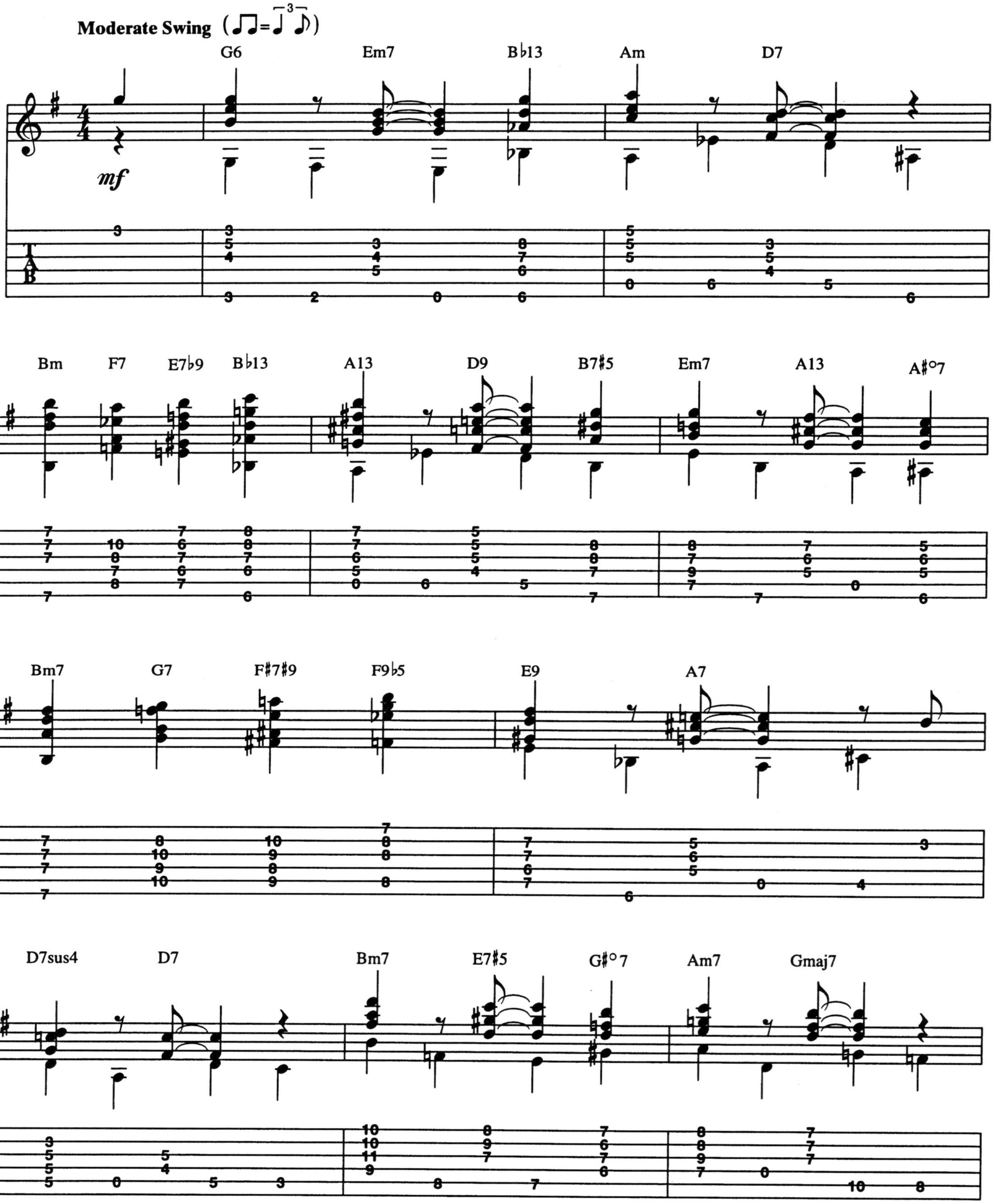

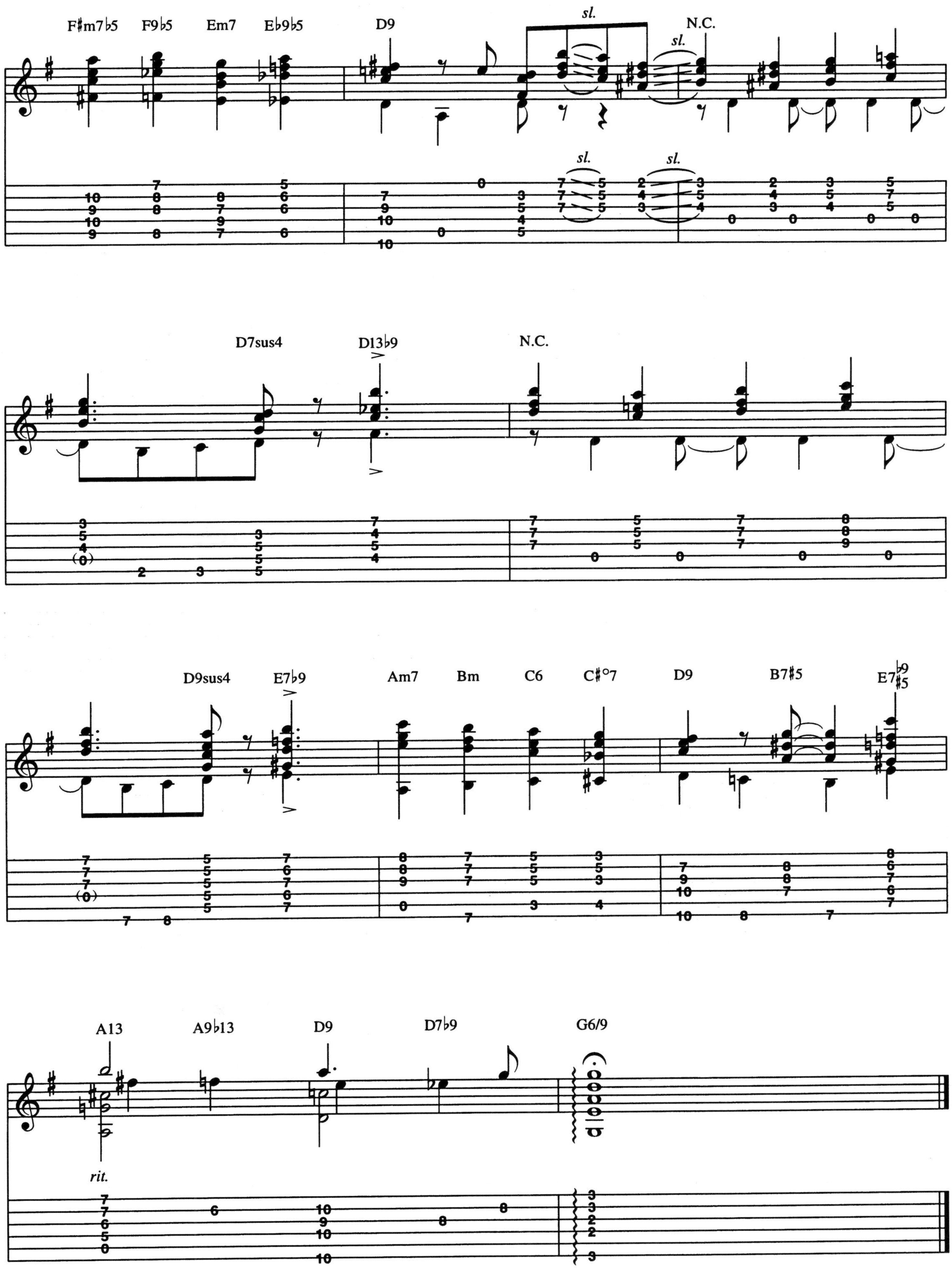
F♯m7♭5 F9♭5 Em7 E♭9♭5 D9 sl. N.C. sl.
sl. sl.
D7sus4 D13♭9 N.C.
D9sus4 E7♭9 Am7 Bm C6 C♯°7 D9 B7♯5 E7♭9♯5
A13 A9♭13 D9 D7♭9 G6/9
rit.

O CHRISTMAS TREE

Traditional German

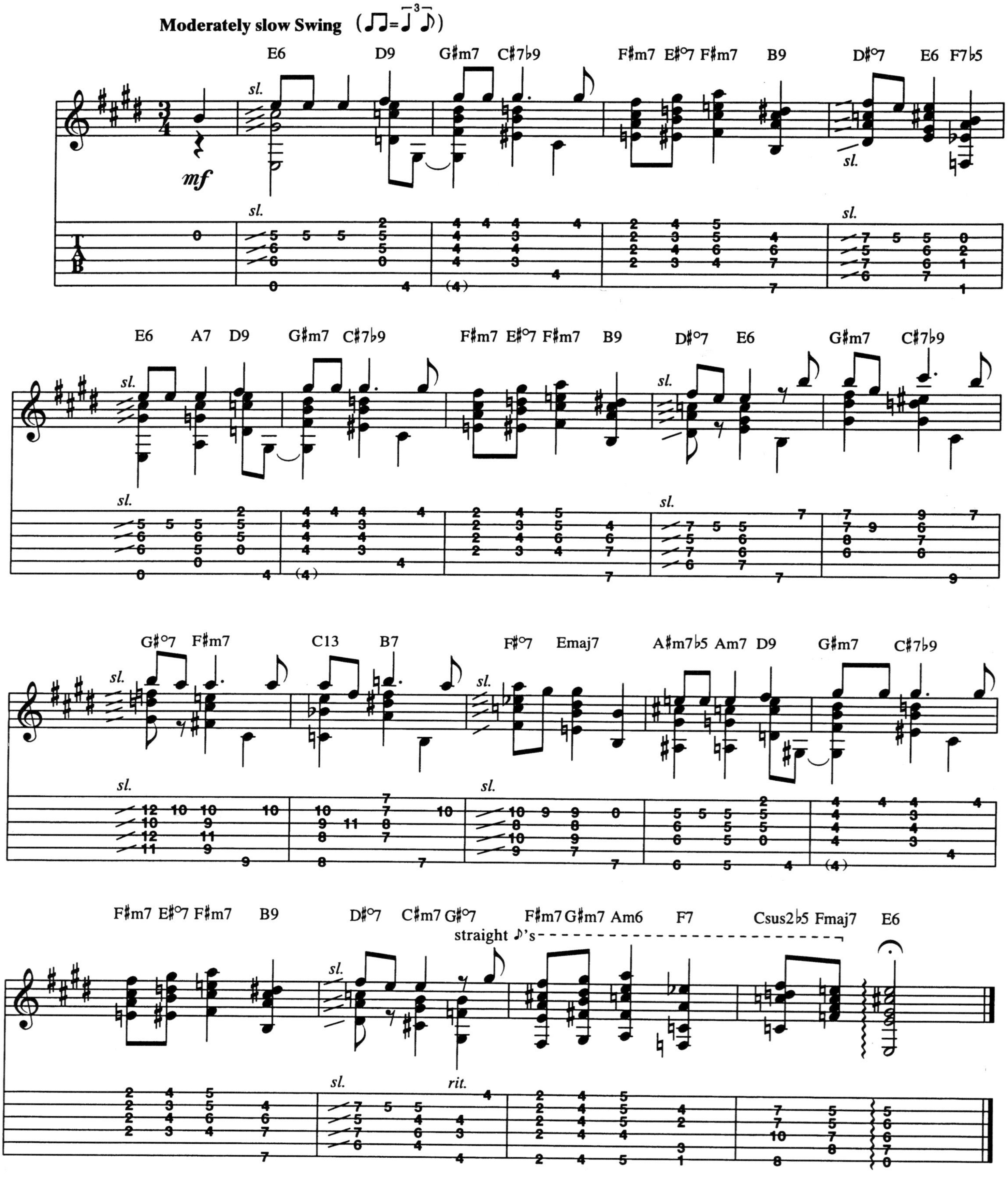

O LITTLE TOWN OF BETHLEHEM

Words by Phillips Brooks
Music by Lewis H. Redner

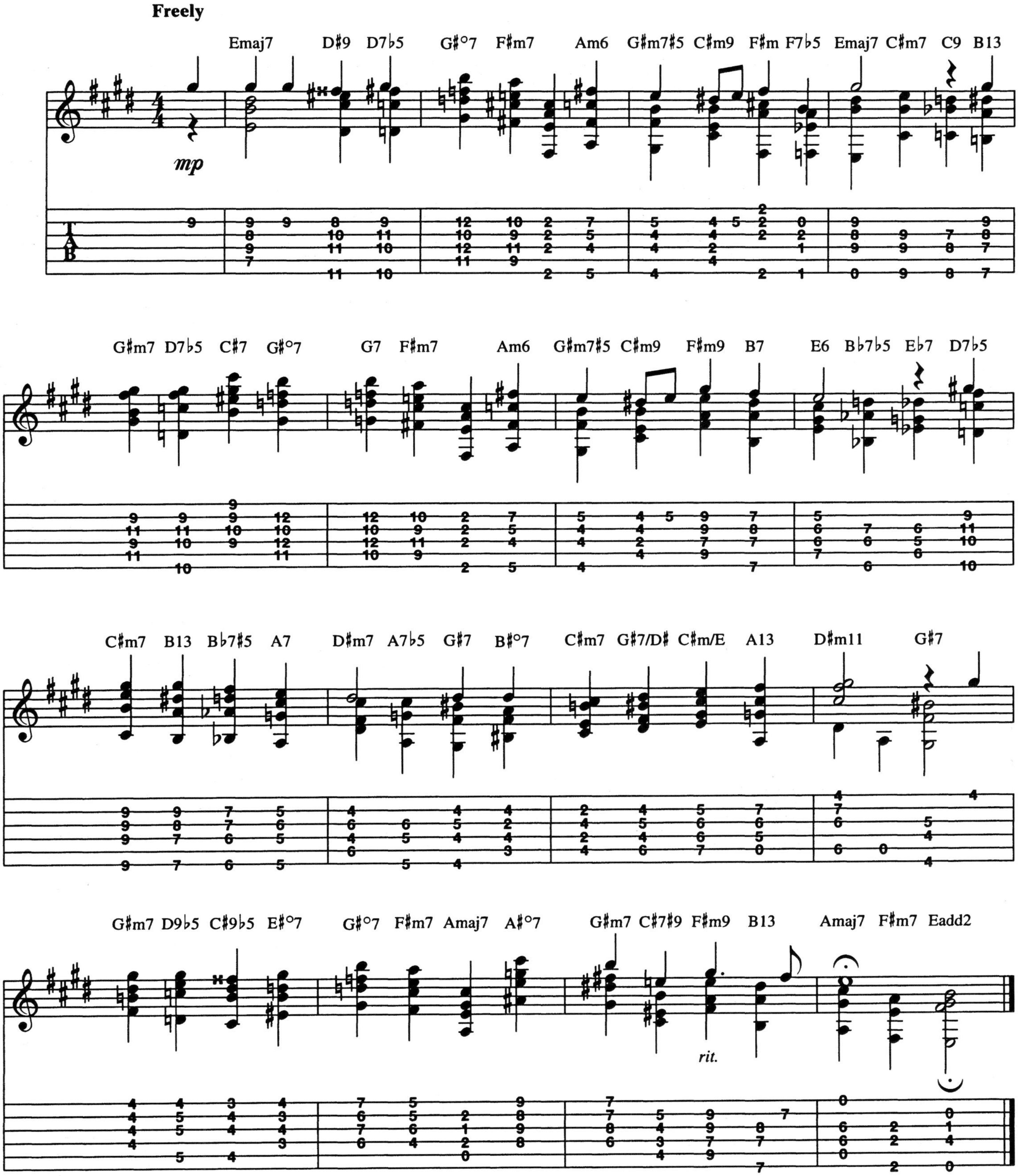

SILENT NIGHT

Words by Joseph Mohr
Music by Franz Gruber

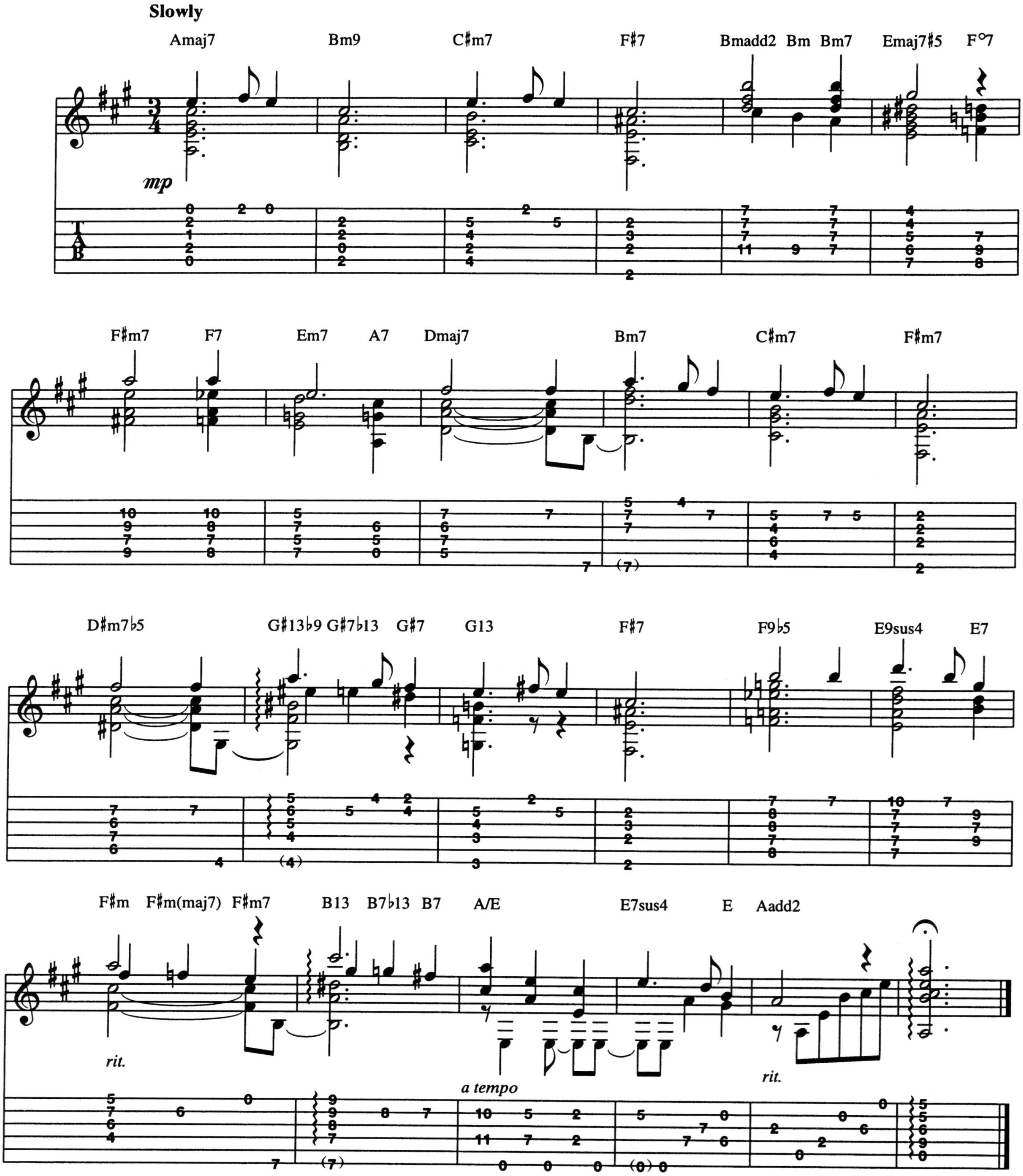

WE THREE KINGS

Words and Music by John Henry Hopkins, Jr.

Moderately upbeat Swing

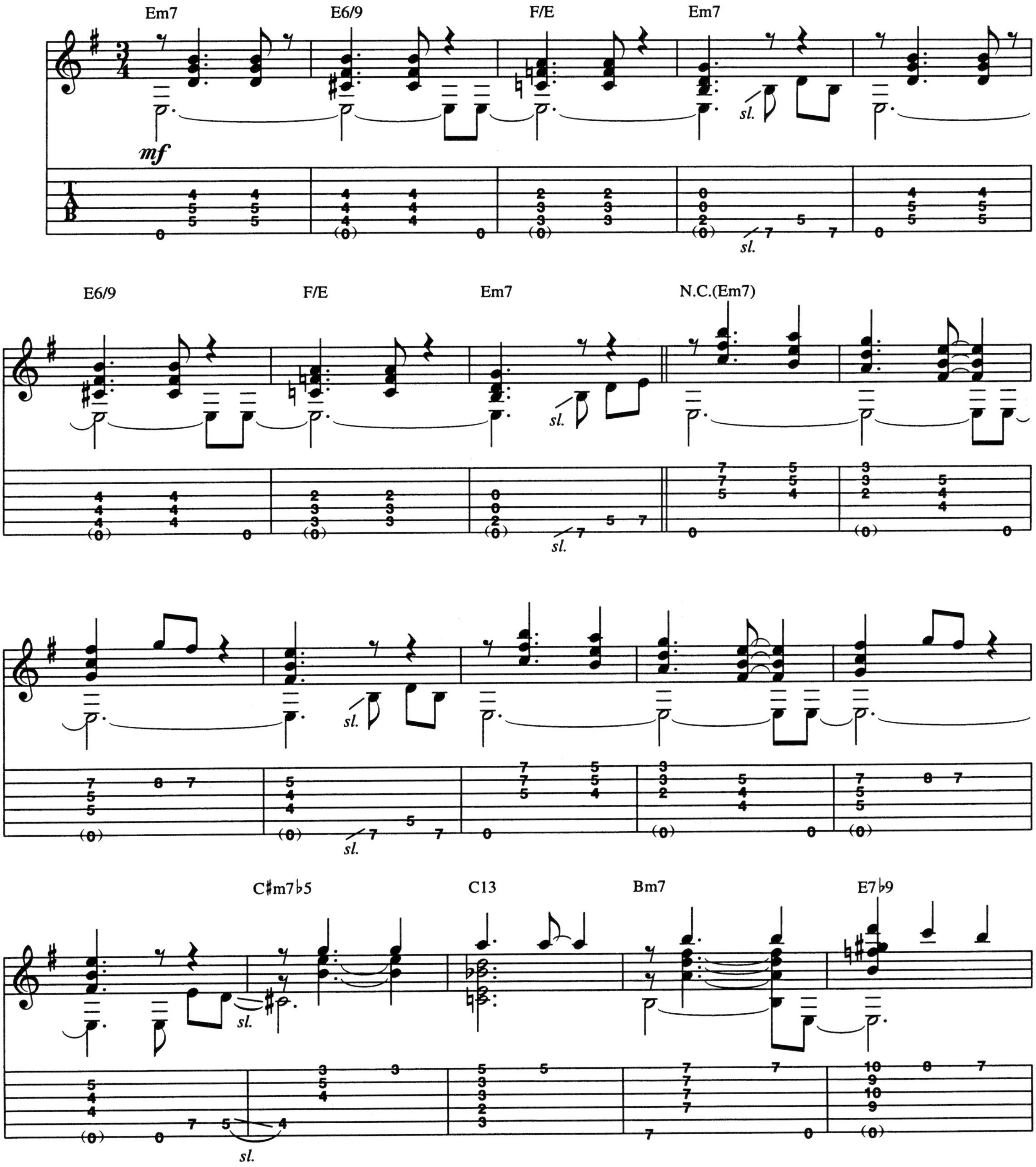

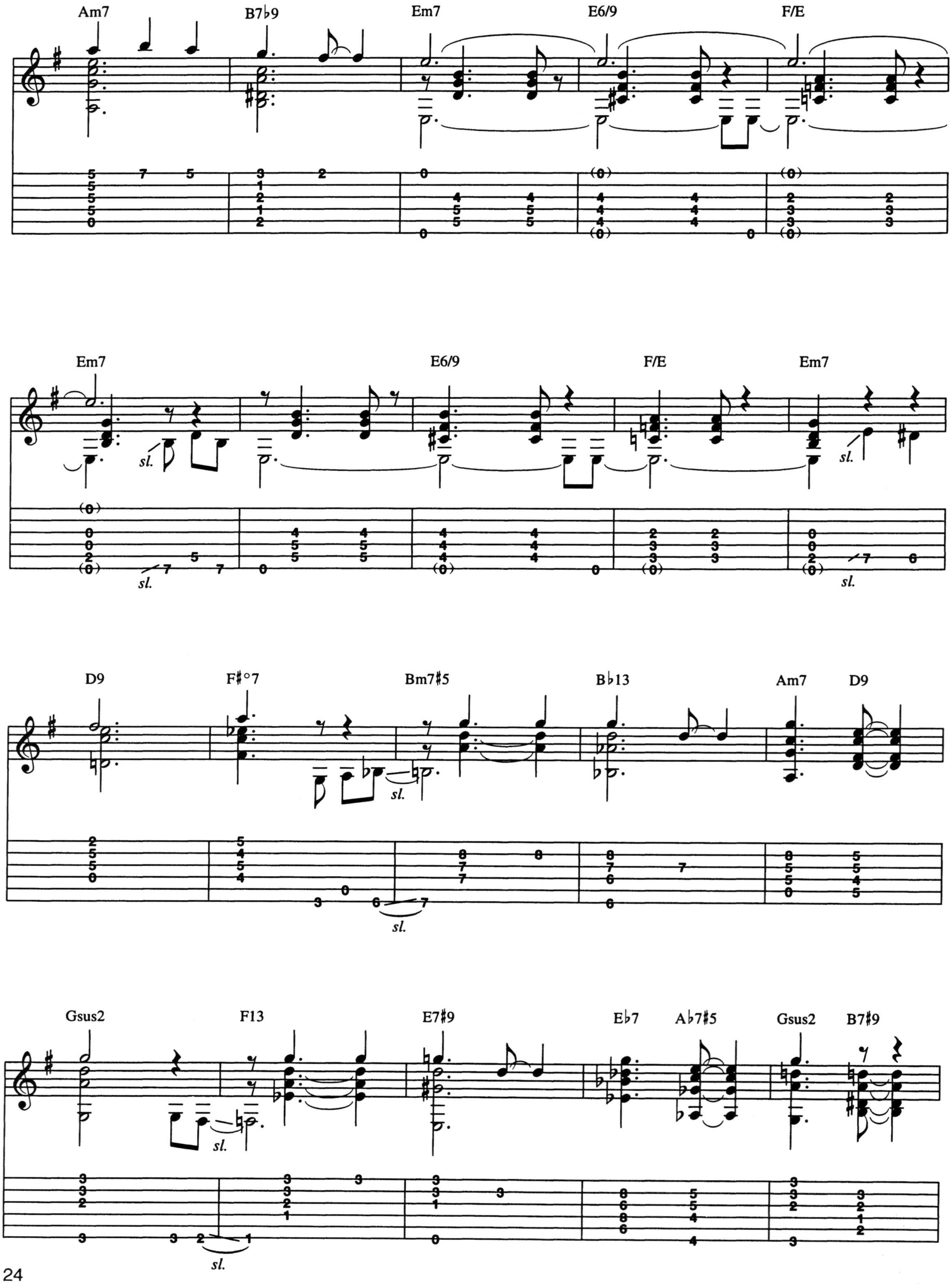
Am7 B7♭9 Em7 E6/9 F/E
Em7 E6/9 F/E Em7
sl.
D9 F♯°7 Bm7♯5 B♭13 Am7 D9
sl.
Gsus2 F13 E7♯9 E♭7 A♭7♯5 Gsus2 B7♯9
sl.

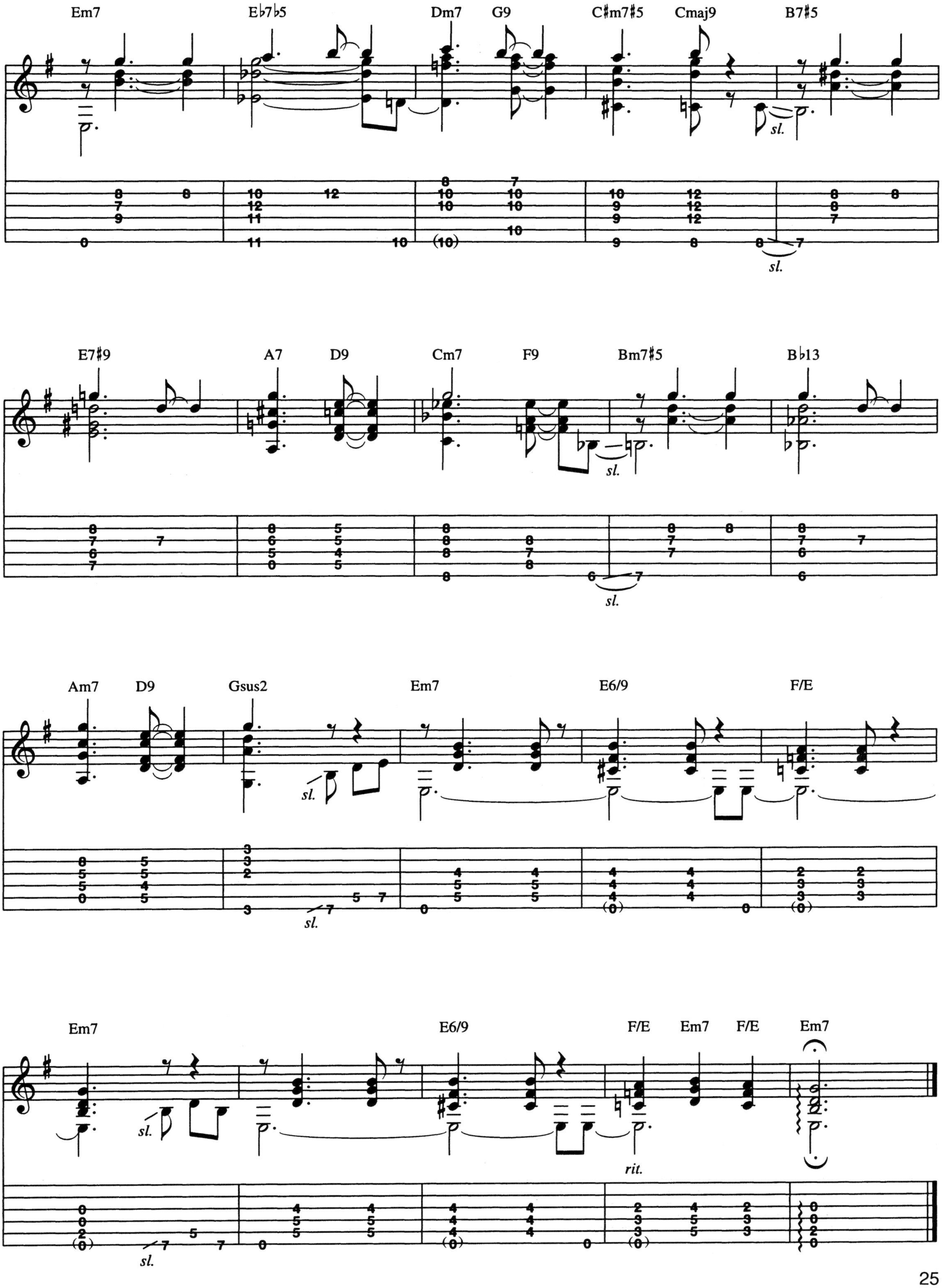
Em7 E♭7♭5 Dm7 G9 C♯m7♯5 Cmaj9 B7♯5
sl.
E7♯9 A7 D9 Cm7 F9 Bm7♯5 B♭13
sl.
Am7 D9 Gsus2 Em7 E6/9 F/E
sl.
Em7 E6/9 F/E Em7 F/E Em7
sl.
rit.

THE FIRST NOËL

French-English

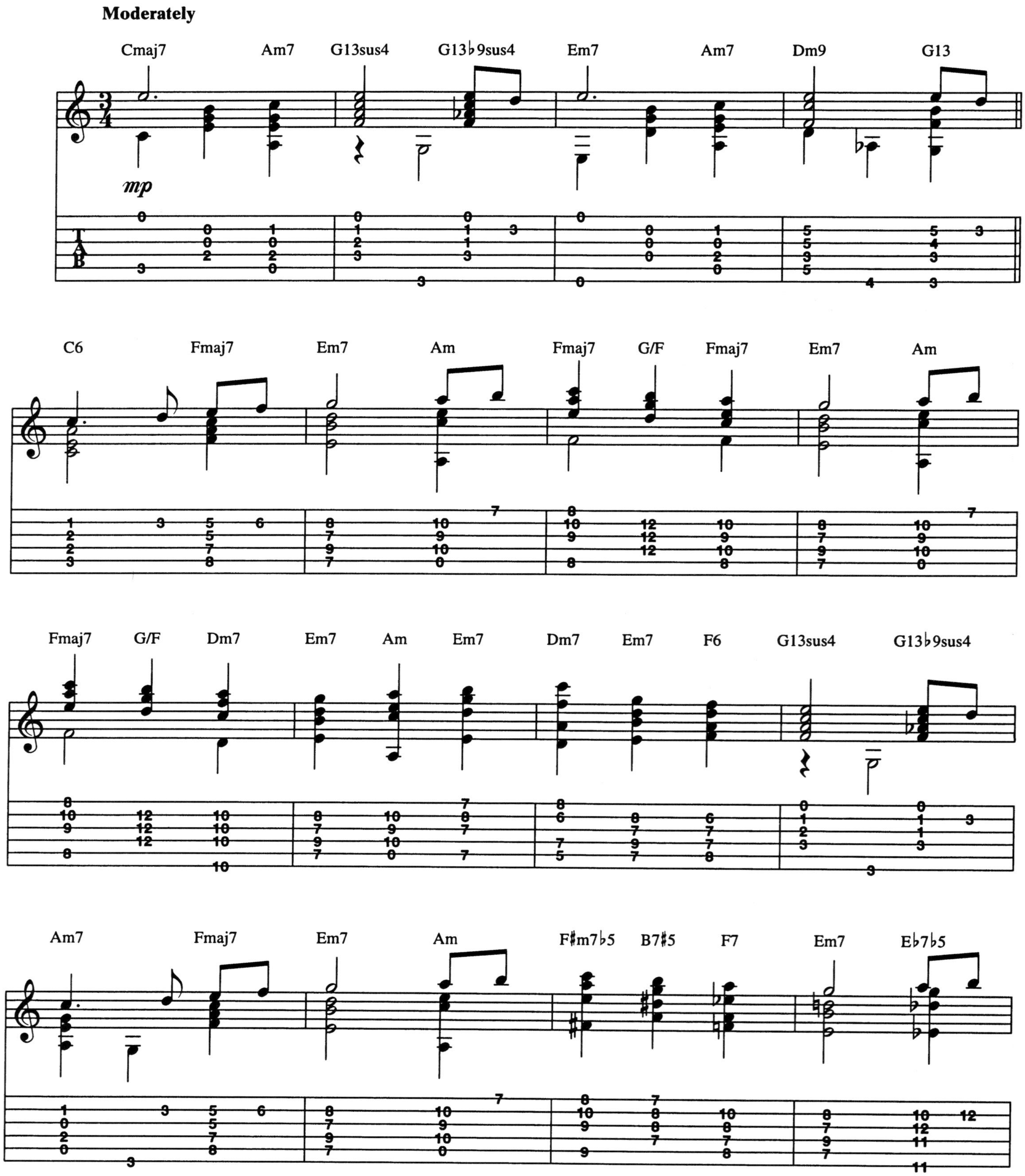

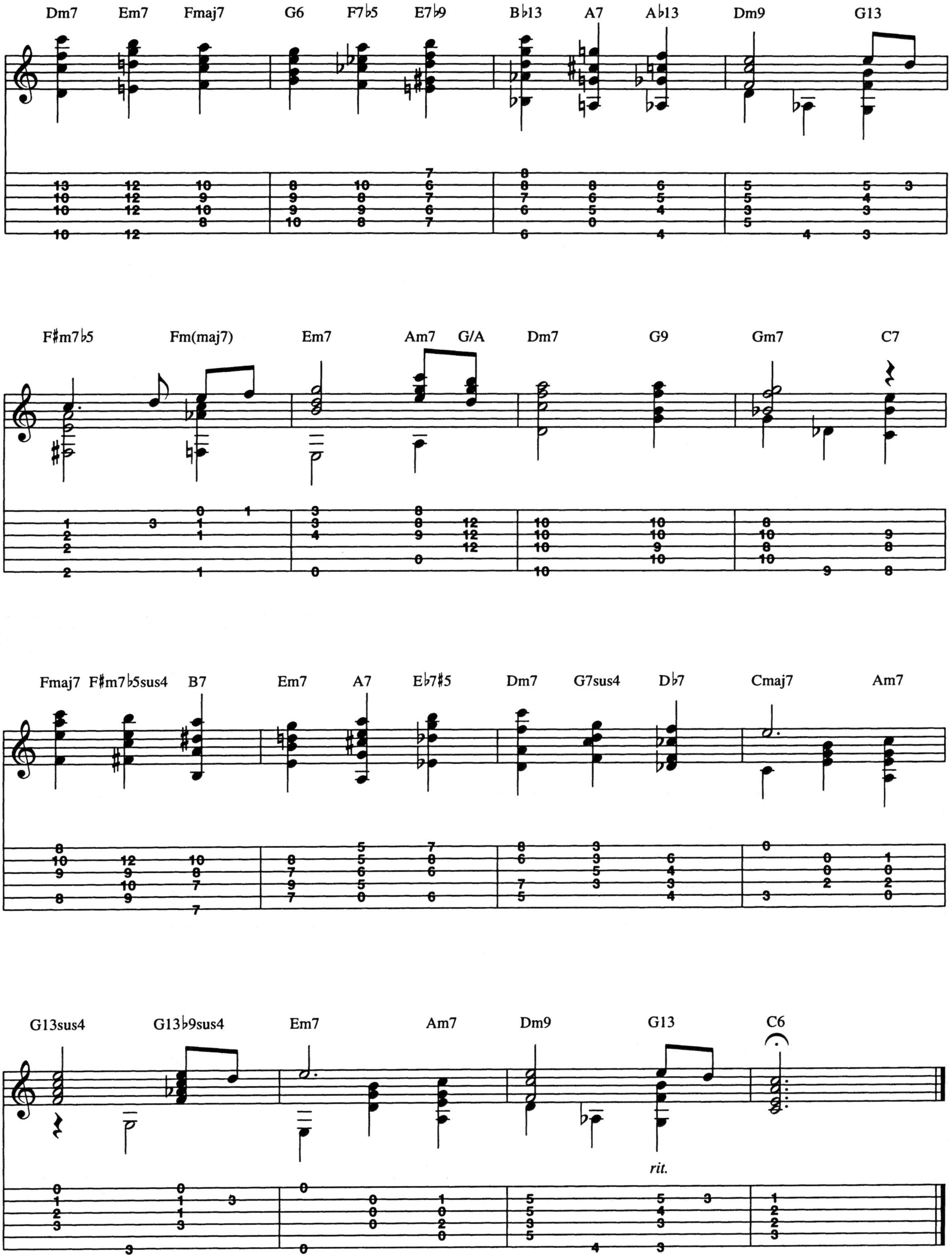
Dm7 Em7 Fmaj7 G6 F7♭5 E7♭9 B♭13 A7 A♭13 Dm9 G13
F♯m7♭5 Fm(maj7) Em7 Am7 G/A Dm7 G9 Gm7 C7
Fmaj7 F♯m7♭5sus4 B7 Em7 A7 E♭7♯5 Dm7 G7sus4 D♭7 Cmaj7 Am7
G13sus4 G13♭9sus4 Em7 Am7 Dm9 G13 C6
rit.

WHAT CHILD IS THIS?

Words by William Chatterton Dix
16th-century English tune "Greensleeves"

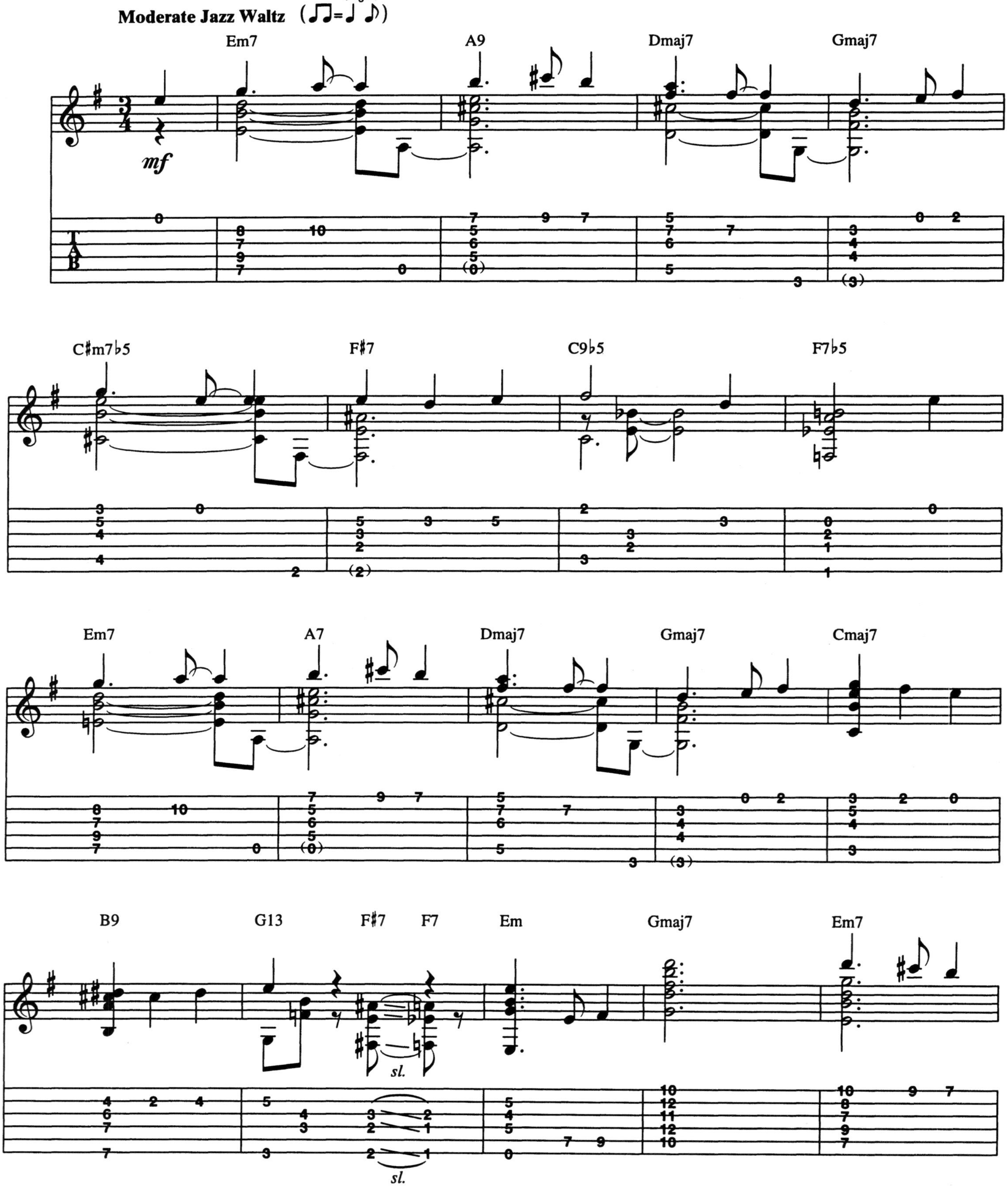

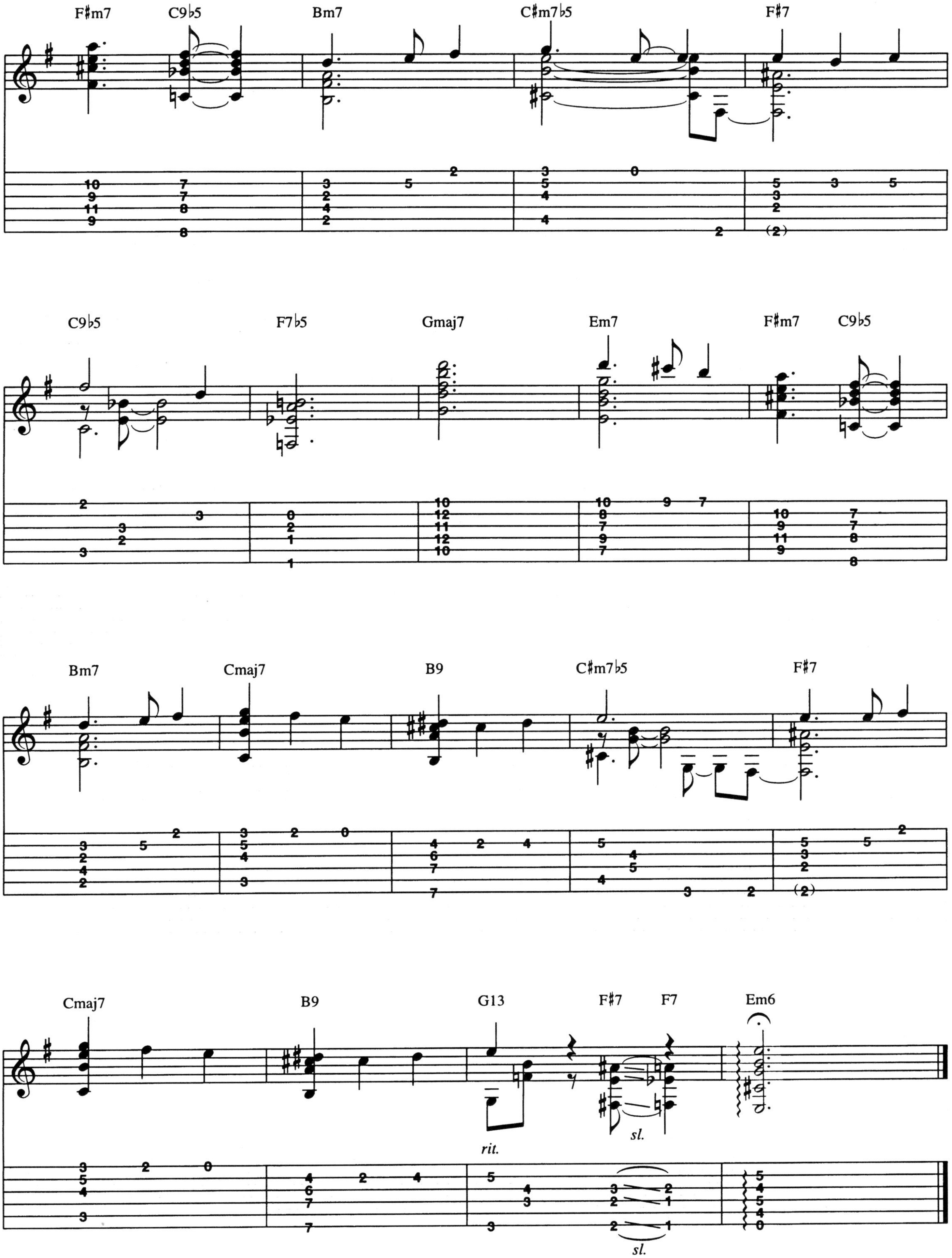
F♯m7 C9♭5 Bm7 C♯m7♭5 F♯7
C9♭5 F7♭5 Gmaj7 Em7 F♯m7 C9♭5
Bm7 Cmaj7 B9 C♯m7♭5 F♯7
Cmaj7 B9 G13 F♯7 F7 Em6
rit.
sl.
sl.

WE WISH YOU A MERRY CHRISTMAS

English Folk Song

Moderately

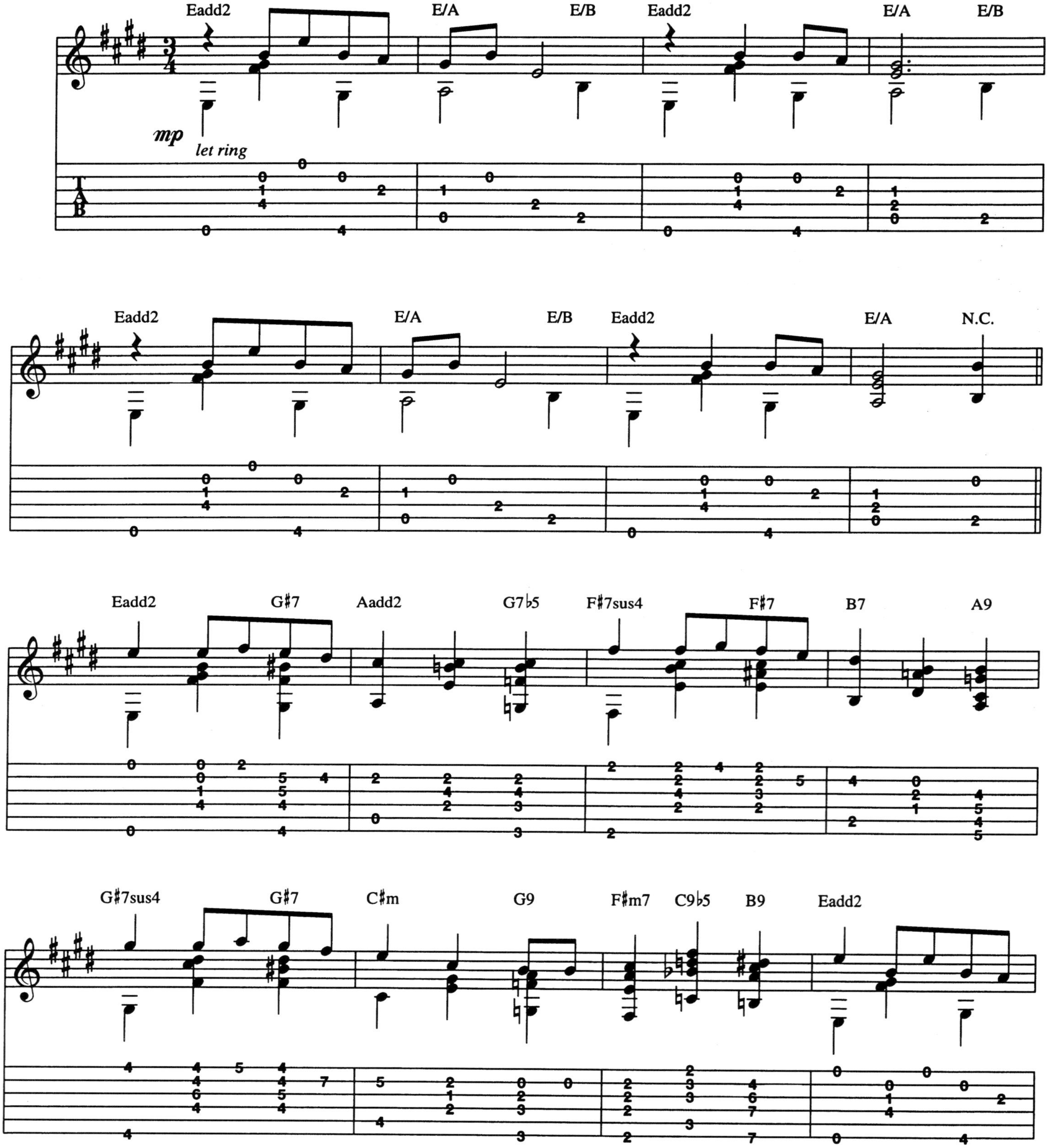

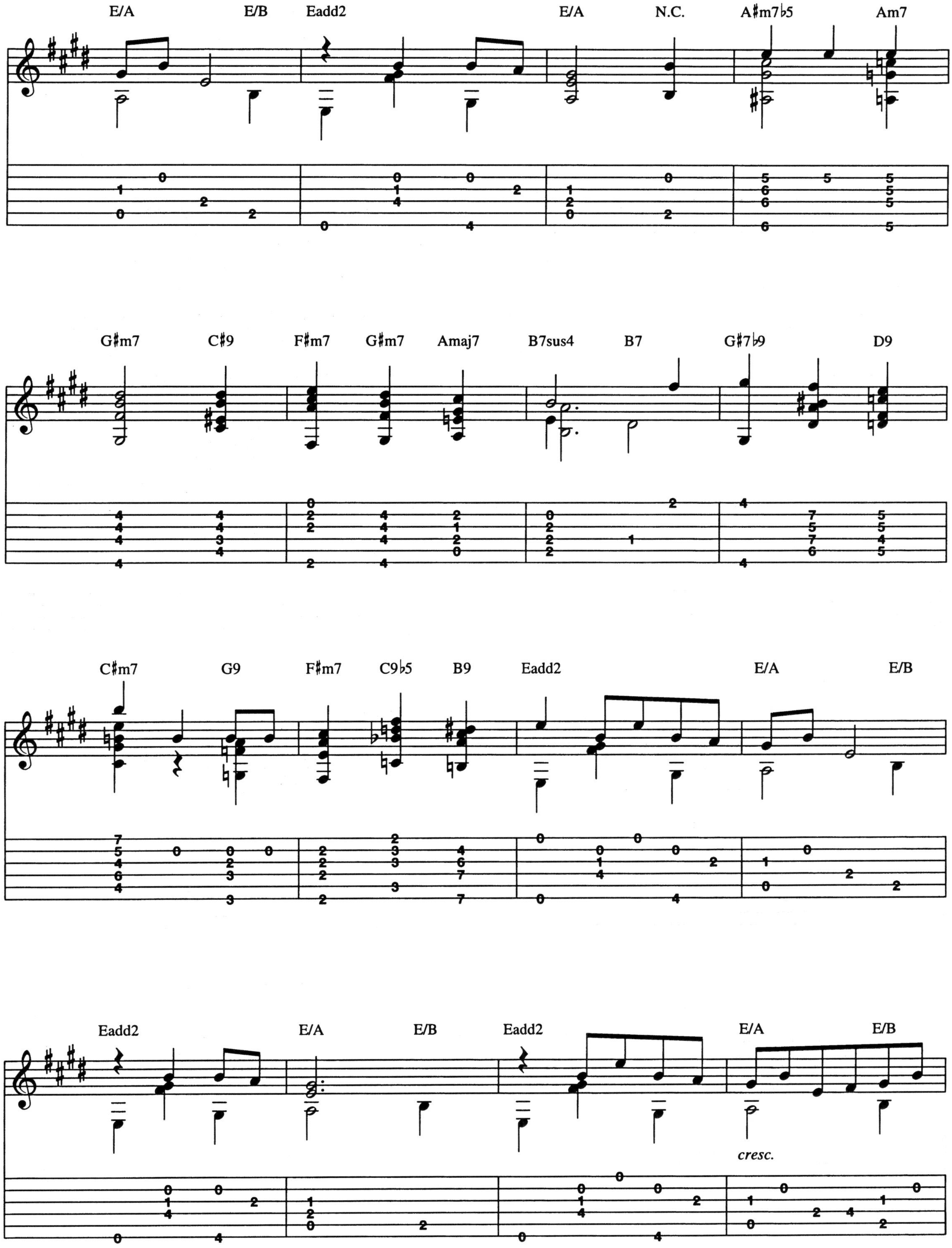
E/A E/B Eadd2 E/A N.C. A♯m7♭5 Am7
G♯m7 C♯9 F♯m7 G♯m7 Amaj7 B7sus4 B7 G♯7♭9 D9
C♯m7 G9 F♯m7 C9♭5 B9 Eadd2 E/A E/B
Eadd2 E/A E/B Eadd2 E/A E/B
cresc.

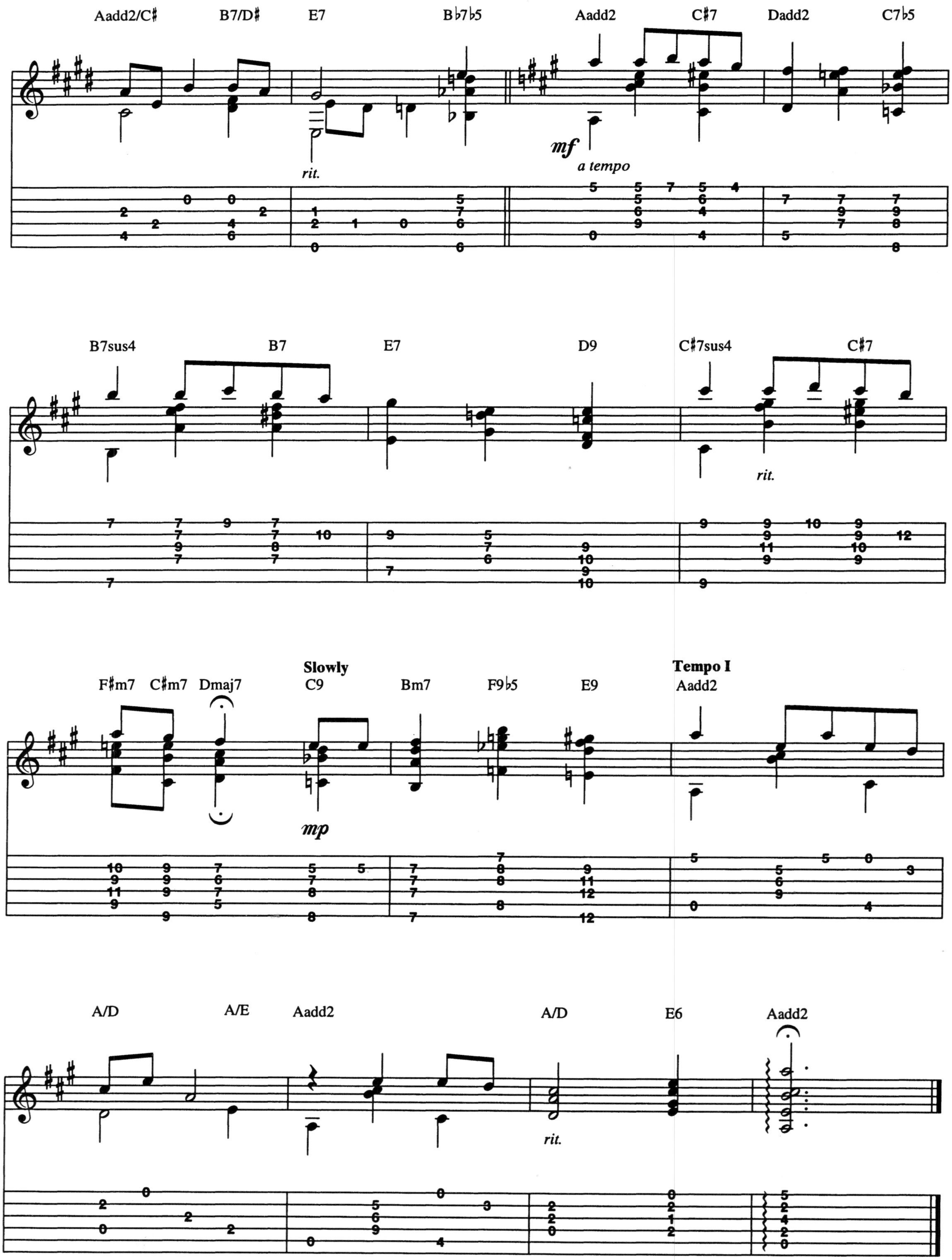
Aadd2/C♯ B7/D♯ E7 B♭7♭5 Aadd2 C♯7 Dadd2 C7♭5
rit.
mf
a tempo
B7sus4 B7 E7 D9 C♯7sus4 C♯7
rit.
Slowly
Tempo I
F♯m7 C♯m7 Dmaj7 C9 Bm7 F9♭5 E9 Aadd2
mp
A/D A/E Aadd2 A/D E6 Aadd2
rit.